THE HIDDEN BILLIONS:
The Potential of the Church in the U.S.A.

Published by C-4 Resources, Inc., 115 N. Neil, Champaign, Illinois 61820, U.S.A.

The Appendix A, Note 2, listing of Virginia Independent City/County Combinations is from *Churches and Church Membership in the United States 1980,* by Bernard Quinn *et al,* copyrighted © 1982 by the National Council of the Churches of Christ in the U.S.A., and reprinted by permission of the Glenmary Research Center.

The Scripture quotations in this publication, unless otherwise indicated, are from the Revised Standard Version of the Bible, copyrighted 1946, 1952, © 1971, 1973 by the Division of Christian Education of the National Council of the Churches of Christ in the U.S.A., and used by permission.

Yoking Map 2: The World cartography by Deborah Lowenherz under the supervision of James Bier, Cartographer, University of Illinois Geography Department, Urbana, Illinois, copyrighted © 1984 by *empty tomb, inc.*

ISBN 0-914527-18-5

Printed in the United States of America by Stipes Publishing Co., Champaign, Illinois.

To our parents
Louis and Doris Slivon

Gladys Ronsvalle
and
Salvatore Ronsvalle

TABLE OF CONTENTS

ACKNOWLEDGMENTS
PREFACE
INTRODUCTION

Table of Contents

LIST OF
TABLES, FIGURES AND MAPS

Tables

ACKNOWLEDGMENTS

There are many people who have provided both talents and love in the production of this book:

Steve Clapp, who as publisher sees clearly into that vast territory between charity ghetto and political penthouse;

Jerry Peterson, who as editor has been creative and encouraging throughout the production process;

Edwin and Dorothy Rae, who had enough confidence in our work to introduce us to Steve Clapp;

Jane Scharf, who joyfully typed all three drafts of the book manuscript;

Caroline Badger, who programmed the necessary computer work for the Yoking Map, and Marion Carter who assisted with regard to the data files;

Larry Thornton, who assisted with the indexing and provided comments on the text with such care.

Ann Shanholtzer and Marleen Geiser, who provided enthusiastic office assistance.

This book reflects an accumulation of years of experiences. We are able to write it because many different Christians in Champaign County, and beyond, too numerous to mention by name, have supported the works through *empty tomb*. The works exist because of their concern. Part of this group includes:

U. Milo and Helen Kaufmann, and John Lee Johnson, who have supported us since the early days of this phase of our journey;

Brad Roos and Ann Shanholtzer, who serve as long-term staff, Pat Wehmer and Joyce Blissit, who have more recently joined the staff, all of whom have helped to make the *empty tomb* works a reality;

W. Howe Donaldson, Jim Boren, Wayne Rogers and Jim Dowd, among other pastors, who have been willing to provide servanthood leadership to the area church in observing all that Christ taught;

the Champaign Mennonite Voluntary Service Unit, who over the years have carried out so much servanthood work;

Bob and Ruth Anderson, and Wilmer and Evelyn Zehr, who have been an inspiration in their commitment to local mission;

the Elkhart CWS/CROP Office folks who have coordinated our Bread from Jesus effort among Catholic Relief Services, Church World Service and World Relief;

Diether Jäckel and the staff of Diaconia, who have most graciously and ably allowed us to assist them in their outreach in Northeast Brazil.

In addition, we acknowledge our neighbors at Bradley Park Apartments who lived through the saga of the sewers.

Finally we think of Ernest Vassar and Bob Koch, who gave us love and support while on earth and who have joined the Hebrews 12 crowd in cheering us on.

We want to express our deep appreciation for each of them and to thank God, the Father, Son and Holy Spirit, for saving us into all the possibilities that following him has provided.

PREFACE

This book is a reflection of the hope we have for the church in the United States. Our experience since 1972 has been that Christians will respond to Jesus' commands to love the poor if specific and clear ways are provided for them to reach out. Buoyed by this positive experience, and given a glorious challenge outlined in the Bible of what it means to follow Jesus, we see no reason not to present clear goals for the church's consideration.

We see every reason to hope that a minimum of 50 percent of the world's population by 1990 or 2000 A.D. would confess Jesus Christ as Lord and Savior. *The World Christian Encyclopedia* (Oxford University Press, New York, 1983) notes that 32 percent of the world's population is Christian now and it projects no change by the year 2000. This mathematical projection, of course, does not take into account the possibility of a mighty outpouring of the Holy Spirit on the world, which manifests itself, in part, in an increased desire in the heart of Christians in the U.S.

Why shouldn't the church in the U.S. set her sights on helping to improve the world's PQLI status, seeing it rise to the 90's, in the next five to fifteen years; PQLI (Physical Quality of Life Index) is based on an average of life expectancy at age one, infant mortality and literacy rates. Recent estimates of PQLI's range from 11 in one African country to 97 in Sweden (the U.S. is 94).

If one is to set goals in the context of the Biblical mandate, why not hope for greater justice and equality among nations as a consequence of richer Christians seeking to share with Christians and non-Christians in need? Given the increasing income available to U.S. Christians since about the time of World War II, this sharing could involve designating $78 billion for overseas word and deed mission, giving tens of billions of dollars to those in need within the U.S., and continuing to operate present congregational programs within the U.S. at their current rate of increase.

Our hopes include the adoption of the Yoking Map that is contained in this book as a viable strategy for developing missions into a vital part of each Christian's discipleship. Individuals and congregations can use the map to help focus their mission concerns while denominations and paradenominational organizations could find it useful in developing their mission strategies. In that vein, our desire would be to make a useful contribution to the ongoing dialogue among denominational and paradenominational mission groups as they seek to be faithful in their word and deed mission outreaches. We hope this book will help provide the church in the U.S. with greater clarity as she considers the implications of Biblical faith. For example, in our opinion Christianity can help us move beyond the currently deadlocked debate of capitalism and communism.

The attempt of U.S. Christians to increase mission efforts is important whether those plans succeed or fail in the short run. Promising ultimate victory, Jesus commands the Christian to try. We do have an honest hope that an obedient church can change things.

It is possible that as the Christians in the U.S. actively pursue some of these goals, not only might world conditions improve but also persecutions may result. Jesus foretold of such persecutions. If so, it will be a comfort to note that the church in the U.S. will not have been guilty of the lukewarmness which will cause Jesus to spit the church of Laodecia out of his mouth.

This discipleship will partly be accomplished by listening to, serving and learning from Christians overseas. Whether any hopes for the church will happen depends in large measure on the choices made by each of the 108,863,089 people in the 375,000 congregations throughout the 3,101 counties in the U.S. as each one attempts to follow God. That's why you as an individual are so important, and why we consider it a privilege to share with you through this book.

John and Sylvia Ronsvalle
Urbana, Illinois

INTRODUCTION

The following chapters outline one approach to applying the Gospel to the evangelism and physical needs of the world. A major theme throughout this book is that God has not only given the church, the body of Christ, the task of addressing the needs of the world but God has also given the church the resources to carry out that task.

This book is written from the perspective of being within the body of Christ in the U.S. It reflects the reality that Christianity in the U.S. is not a state-established religion and yet has widespread support. The book encompasses the increasing incomes of a majority of U.S. citizens over the last forty years. And it addresses the cooperation necessary and possible among Christians from different traditions when no one denomination is recognized as the predominant Christian faith.

The Hidden Billions has three sections. In Part I, personal experiences with domestic and international concerns provide background for some of the conclusions and suggestions presented in this book.

Specific strategies are outlined in Part II. The personal focus of relationships between richer Christians and poorer Christians and non-Christians translates into local and international strategies for sharing the large income available to Christians in the U.S.A.

Part III contains an exploration of general concepts and ideas with a concluding chapter focusing on specific suggestions and general hope regarding the church's task on earth. These concepts range from the possibility of applying the above strategies, to the interrelationships of the kingdoms of Capitalism, Communism and God.

PART I

PART I

Beginning to think about the potential of the church in the U.S.A. means that we Christians must encounter certain important but difficult concepts. Chapter 1 presents the reader not only with facts which involve huge numbers — actually billions — but also puts these facts in a societal as well as Biblical context.

In Chapter 2, a first-hand account of two, educated middle-class whites moving into an all-black, low-income housing project is recounted. Our purpose in moving into such a neighborhood was to be a link of communication. Our hope was to explore additional ways by means of which richer Christians could pursue justice with poorer Christians, and then together reach out to poorer non-Christians. What resulted was a two and a half year journey through a maze of bureaucracy, while trying to get raw sewage off people's floors. The link to the broader Christian community became a vital part of the solution.

The involvement of some U.S. Christians with a specific area of need in the world is reviewed in Chapters 3 and 4. This experience has meant that "world poverty" has been translated into the struggles that people named José, Antonio and Epitacio face. The personal focus has meant that Jesus' command to care about the poor begins to have a specific as well as general application.

Finally, Chapter 5 reflects on the question of why the richer Christian should seek out personal experiences with the poor in the first place.

CHAPTER 1

Facing the Task

A quick quiz

What do the following statistics have in common:

— Almost one billion (1,000,000,000) people go to bed hungry every night.
— 2.5 billion people have never had an adequate presentation of the Gospel of Jesus Christ.
— It costs billions of dollars each year to address poverty in the United States.
— Experts estimate that $4 billion each year over the next 15 years, if spent effectively, could eliminate world hunger by the year 2000 A.D.[1]
— The difference between current church giving levels (1.6 percent per capita) and the amount of money available to church outreach if giving were 10 percent per capita, is over $100 billion per year.

What do these statistics have in common? Well, first each statistic above involves billions.

A billion.

That's a number that is hard to think about. For the average lay reader these statistics become meaningless. It's hard to imagine a billion anything.

Hidden facts

The second common point is that each of these facts barely touches the typical person's daily life, if indeed there is any contact at all. Poor people overseas appear in Sunday newspaper photograph layouts, on the news between a bomb explosion and a new athletic feat, or are talked about from the pulpit on special offering Sundays. The unevangelized are preached about in some congregations and debated in others. Generally, world changing is considered to be in the realm of governments. Residents of one neighborhood feel comfortable with the local poor living invisibly across town and church giving is only conveniently mentioned in the annual steward-ship drive. As a result, all of these facts are "hidden" from most of us as we live our daily lives.

God cares

Third, the Bible addresses all these topics in various forms. John 3:16 notes that God sent his Son for the whole world, while 1 Timothy 2:4 asserts that it is God's will that all would be "saved and come to a knowledge of the truth." Jesus continues the Old Testament theme of caring for the poor, the oppressed, the widows and orphans in parables and statements in the New Testament. He uncomfortably raises the issue in Matthew 25 as to whether in fact his followers know God if they are not feeding, clothing, visiting, liberating those in need. Money and its responsible use, some say, is the second most talked about theme in the Bible, following idolatry. Considering that Paul equates greed with idolatry in Colossians 3:5, use of financial resources apparently is a topic close to God's heart.

Finally, then, anything that is important to God, as evidenced by repeated mention in the Bible, ought to be a real concern to every Christian. This conclusion presents a problem. If these facts are not only hidden from our daily lives but also hard to think about when we confront them, how is the Christian supposed to be faithful in this area of addressing financial resources and world need? God's strength being perfected in our weakness, maybe the Christian should begin by admitting that these ideas are difficult and removed from him or her and then proceed by grace, a step at a time. That is certainly how we began our journey.

CHAPTER 2

Love Your Neighbor — Across Town

Move to public housing?

The idea did not easily occur to us that we could, as a white couple from middle-class backgrounds, move into Bradley Park Apartments, an all-black, low income housing project in Champaign, Illinois, by ourselves. The idea that did appeal to us was buying the boarded up project across the street from Bradley Park, moving in with five other couples and living among the poor in the context of a somewhat controlled, Christian community base. Since we never found more than one or two people who even *liked* this idea at the same time, the community never materialized. And our plans to purchase the boarded up projects were ended when a person working with the Bradley Park Tenants Organization asked us to stop in deference to their attempt to buy the buildings.

We thought our future in low-income housing was over.

Slowly, however, the conviction grew that the two of us not only *could* move into Bradley Park, but that we *should*. So we did — on Halloween, 1980. We hoped God was giving us a treat and not a trick.

Our new surroundings

The complex consists of ten residential buildings and one office-laundromat building. There are eight sets of townhouses, each building containing four to seven units. These townhouses have three to four bedrooms and often house six to fifteen family members. We moved into the first floor of one of the two twenty-four unit apartment buildings. The apartments have one or two bedrooms, with eight apartments on the first floor.

As soon as we knew we were planning to move into Bradley Park, we began mentioning it to people who came to our outreach house at empty tomb, inc. for clothes or food. We hoped in this way to be somewhat known among the tenants before we moved in. Nevertheless, some people seemed to come to their windows to watch us walk to and from our apartment the first week we lived there. And once there were two boys wrestling. They stopped to watch us as we walked by.

"They live here," one said, not taking his eyes off us.

"They do not!" the other replied, amazed. "Do Toos" and "Do Nots" exchanged as they began to wrestle again.

As we moved in, one young boy came up to our open window and began a conversation: Did we live here? Did we go to church? Did we know a lot of people got killed here? It was interesting to see how he thought about the place in which he lived.

We settled into public housing. The apartment itself was very nice. There was a living room, dining area, kitchen, a bedroom and bath with shower and tub. There were also the stereotyped ghetto problems. The windows streamed in air (plastic helped stem that). Roaches happily shared our quarters (boric acid seemed to help). The heating registers were in the ceiling so the warm air stood six feet from the floor in the winter. And a 2 foot by 1 foot spot in the carpeting was rotted out. We viewed all these circumstances as adding to the authenticity of our surroundings.

What's that on the floor?

Then we came home on Palm Sunday, 1981 to find our carpet "squishy" wet. There had been a fire in the building in which no one was hurt, fortunately. We reported the wet carpet to the manager who informed us that the water was not from fire hoses. The water was from the sanitary sewers which regularly backed up on people's floors in the complex. In fact, that was why the carpet in our hall had rotted out. It had been flooded so often with raw sewage water that it finally rotted away.

We went back to our apartment, dumbfounded. In the utility room we found a pipe in the floor from which the overflows came. Sure enough, around it was used toilet tissue and evidence of actual sewage waste.

We contacted the Tenants Organization President. She explained that the organization had been talking to management for years with no response. We spoke with our upstairs neighbor, a gentle woman with gray hair, who said she had lived in the complex for nine years and overflows had happened the whole time she was there. She said, in fact, she had gone to the City Council in 1974 only to be told it was not in the City's jurisdiction.

We contacted the apartment manager who confirmed that the overflows happened regularly. He had protested the problem to the United States Department of Housing and Urban Development (HUD), the owner at that time, who had consistently told him that the problem would be too expensive to fix.

We contacted the City Manager who said he, also, had contacted HUD to complain about the matter. A HUD representative told the City Manager that if the City tried to make the overflows a public issue, HUD might decide to close the complex down. With a tight housing market, the City Manager explained he could not risk losing 98 units of low income housing.

We contacted a HUD official who expressed surprise that the carpets had rotted out due to the overflows. He called back two days later, proudly stating that he had arranged for the carpets to be replaced with floor tiles so that the overflows would be easier for the tenants to clean up. HUD officials continued to insist that the problem was tenant abuse of the system. A City official who became interested took an unofficial survey of City code enforcement staff, engineers and others familiar with the situation. The consensus was that "those people" were making their own problems.

A call to the church

Over a period of years, our work has brought us into contact with churches throughout the county. We finally appealed to the county church people through our regular newsletter. Several individuals contacted us and we formed a committee. The committee established that a housing project across the street with similar tenants and density did not have similar sewer backups. We checked rain figures to establish that rainfall did not correspond to the backups. We looked through old records and came across the name of an original inspecting architect. It turned out that one of the committee members fed the architect's son brownies and milk when he came over to see her son after school. We therefore were able to get the only extant set of plans for the complex.

As the relationship networked out of the committee, we were able to talk with a City official whose wife was the Girl Scout leader of a committee member's daughter, and a City Council member whose daughter lived down the block from another committee member. Letters were written to the U.S. Senators and the local U.S. Representative, and the City Council even passed a resolution stating its concern after receiving contacts from church people who lived all over the community. After a press release, the town newspaper and the local TV and radio stations reported the facts we uncovered.

Finally, the City paid for a sanitary engineering study which concluded, fourteen months after we had begun the investigation, that in fact the pipes had been laid wrong in construction. The question was not why the sewer backed up, said the engineer, but why the pipes worked at all. For ten years, the cause of the overflows had not been the tenants' abuse of the system but no slope in the pipes.

HUD first accepted the study results, then rejected the study, then proposed an alternative experimental solution rather than the recommended replacement of the sewer lines.

Back to the church

For ten years we in *empty tomb* had been contacting church people, inviting them to help feed the hungry, share used furniture and clothing, do home repair for those unable to keep their homes up. Now we asked these Christians to express their concern to the City Council members on behalf of the Bradley Park residents who were vulnerable to these sewer overflows. As a result, the City negotiated and HUD finally agreed, after seven months, to arrange for five of the ten defective sewer lines to be replaced.

We went back to the churches again, presenting them with the facts of why ten sewer lines should be replaced. The local newspaper and TV and radio stations covered the developments. In two weeks, a petition requesting that ten sewer lines be replaced was passed around in 36 county congregations. Christians who would be considered to be on the extremely conservative end of the church spectrum and Christians from the liberal end both expressed their concern because of Jesus' concern. A petition with 2,284 signatures was presented to the Chicago and Washington offices of HUD, to the two U.S. Senators from Illinois and the local U.S. Representative, as well as to denominational leaders whose local adherents had contributed signatures.

The U.S. Senators continued to express concern and a month later, the U.S. Representative's Office announced that negotiations had produced a HUD commitment to replace eight of the ten sewers.

As of this writing, we do not consider the matter settled. Throughout the two and a half years, we felt like we were following the pillar of cloud and fire as the Israelites did in the wilderness. Now we wait in faith to see what steps we feel God is directing us to take.

Links lead to solution

The significance of this story, however, is not "making the system work." The important fact to note is that a whole group of people, Christians and non-Christians, within a town were subjected to unhealthy, unsafe, disgusting living conditions for ten years because they were too poor to move away. And the societal prejudice had isolated the people so completely that they could not make contact with anyone willing to change the situation. Prejudice ran so strongly against them that everyone in a position to help the tenants assumed the overflows were the tenants' fault. The structural defect finding was a strong vindication of the tenants but a terrible comment on the destructive isolation present in our society. How many children grew up with a self-image that said society-at-large felt it was OK for them to have raw sewage on their floors? How many children in this complex concluded that the churched half of this society was also saying, during those ten years, that it was OK for those kids to live with raw sewage on their floors? And if the church thought it was OK, did Jesus think so too?

The situation could have gone on for ten more years except that a linkage out to the larger society resulted from a simple step of obedience. It becomes apparent that Jesus was expressing more than a simple platitude when he said, "Love your neighbor as yourself." We may want the good for our neighbor, but we probably want the best for ourselves. And now it was our carpet, as well as our neighbors', that squished with sewage water. We were able to interpret the need to the larger church community and the church expressed its concern. God can act powerfully through the church when the church is presented with the facts and then is willing to respond in obedience.

CHAPTER 3

Love Your Neighbor — Overseas

A common mission

Overseas missions seemed distant and not vital to a variety of people in Champaign County, Illinois in 1976. Again and again, the comment was made that while congregation members were willing to support denominational mission programs, people felt their enthusiasm would increase if there was an opportunity to learn in a first-hand way what the conditions were overseas and to grow in the understanding of how sent gifts were used.

So there was strong support when a cooperative, trans-denominational mission effort was suggested. The idea was simple. Christians in Champaign County would cooperate on a second-mile giving project, beyond current denominational giving, which would send gifts to a certain area of the world. While emphasis was placed on the need for the overseas national Christians to take the initiative in defining needs and solutions in this mission project, end-use reports would be requested by the Champaign County Christians. The purpose of such end-use information (how gifts are used at the distribution end) was not so much to check up on the use of the gifts as to provide information with which to educate the U.S. Christians.

The project was strengthened by its association with *empty tomb* in two ways. First, the majority of *empty tomb* works focused on local need. By an overseas mission project being couched among local outreaches, the confusing debate of local mission vs. overseas mission was minimized.

Second, since 1972 the focus of *empty tomb* had been on the entire body of Christ, or church, in an area. This idea is built on the New Testament record of Christians being regarded as members of a church in an area (Letter to the Colossians, Philippians, Romans as well as Jesus addressing the church at various cities in the first three chapters of The Revelation). Also, Jesus' prayer in John 17, for the oneness of his followers, seems to indicate the fact that Christians cooperating will have an evangelistic impact on those around the church, "so that they will believe you sent me." It was natural, therefore, to invite all county congregations with an historical confession of Christ to join the project.

Selecting an area

Recognizing the denominational reality of most of the participating congregations, the administrative endorsement of three mission agencies was sought and received: Catholic Relief Services (Roman Catholic Church), Church World Service (National Council of Churches) and World Relief Commission (National Association of Evangelicals). The thinking was that if the gifts could be distributed in an area where all three mission groups were active, and through a national Christian agency with which all felt comfortable, then Champaign County Christians could feel confident that their gifts were being used in a way compatible with their profession of faith.

To find such a geographical location, we went to Church World Service (CWS). The area of Northeast Brazil was suggested to us. Brazil is a country where 90 percent of the people are Catholic. A Protestant Brazilian group, Diaconia, coordinated the mission outreach of seven Protestant denominations. The projects were initiated by leaders in the communities and therefore, almost always, the Diaconia projects were assisting Catholic community leaders. A working ecumenism was thus in operation.

Learning as we go

In 1977 the Champaign County churches attempted to send wheat flour to Northeast Brazil for distribution by Diaconia. The first thing we learned about Brazil was the reality of infrastructure. The wheat flour ended up in the south and could not be transported 2,000 miles overland to the north, so Diaconia distributed the flour in the south. That turned out to be just as well because the preference is for cornmeal in the north.

For two more years we shipped cornmeal, each time getting to the right port. We had to listen very closely, however, to our Brazilian brother in Christ when we got a polite letter from Diaconia suggesting that there was some difficulty in distributing boxcarloads of cornmeal. The suggestion was made that cash gifts could be put to better use since water was in critical shortage. Wells and sanitation projects could use cash gifts more productively than the cornmeal could be distributed.

We Champaign County Christians were having to learn at a fast rate. One repeated question from those contributing money was how did we know the gifts were really getting to the poor and not lining some politicians' pockets? If people were doubtful about cornmeal being misused, wouldn't they be really concerned about money?

Growing as we learn

It is a credit to both the Champaign County Christians and the Brazilian Christians that this transition from goods to cash took place with a minimum of difficulty.

The Brazilian Christians in Diaconia normally gave contributors financial reports and progress reports. Therefore, it would have been easy for them to interpret our extra emphasis on end-use as a lack of trust. They chose instead to trust us. Also, the Diaconia Superintendent was most patient and sympathetic with our discussions and our requests for information and rationale about the switch from product to money.

The Champaign County Christians raised good questions about the use of any money we sent. The Coordinating Committee explained the fact that although we U.S. Christians had resources to share, we could not possibly know the situation or understand the needs as well as our Brazilian brothers and sisters in Christ. Assurances were given that there was strong concern on both sides of the project that the money would be responsibly used. The basic issue came down to whether Champaign Christians would trust Brazilian Christians. Presented with the facts, the Champaign County Christians "grew up into Christ" a little more and affirmed that taking the lead from Brazil was the right way to go. The money we sent has assisted in sanitation (outhouses, wells), a health outpost, dam construction and Bible distribution.

The discussions were awkward at times but proved to help build increased understanding between those of us in Champaign County and the Christians in Brazil. Therefore, we had to take very seriously the suggestion from Brazil that a delegation come to visit to see the projects firsthand and meet the Diaconia staff face-to-face.

The logical people to go included the *empty tomb* staff working with the project. The whole project was John's brain-child and Sylvia served as daily coordinator. But we also had the most reservations about going. Even if we could get on a charter flight going to the area and keep our expenses to a minimum, wouldn't the $1,000 per person be better spent on actual projects rather than a trip? The other Coordinating Committee members prevailed. After all, wasn't one purpose of the project to really promote better understanding? How much longer could both sides go on only exchanging money and end-use reports and really feel like partners? So the churches in Champaign County sent a delegation of four people, consisting of a Franciscan nun, who worked with the Acre Phase, a former Mennonite Missionary, who served as translator, and the two of us. Our task: to bring greetings from the Christians in Champaign County, and to learn as much as we could.

CHAPTER 4

Love Your Neighbor —
Whose Children Are Dying

Recife, Pernambuco State, Brazil

Flying to Northeast Brazil, what should one expect to see? We knew it was a drought region. The outhouses our money helped build in the rural area were an improvement over the bushes. We knew few if any people in the villages we helped had running water — and even then it might be turned on only for an hour a day. What kind of city could there be if such village conditions existed only 80 miles to the west?

As it turned out, we found a very cosmopolitan city. Recife has a population of one and a half million. Tall modern buildings contrast with classic Portuguese architecture. Our first impression was afforded by the bustle of cars leaving the crowded airport. The airport terminal was open-air. How impractical, was the first thought — what do they do when it snows? Ah, came the amused second thought, since we were 100 miles south of the equator, snow was not a reality.

We learned right away, though, what it was like to live in a city where 70 percent of the people are really poor: we did not stop for any red lights. To halt at a stop light at night, we were told, is an invitation for robbery. Petty theft was a serious problem. The decorative grill work on windows and doors served a practical purpose as well.

While in the city we chose to stay at a Catholic orphanage rather than a hotel. The 100 little girls were charming and the head nun made us feel like special guests. We learned that the orphanages could only house a small percentage of the 100,000 abandoned children in Recife. So, four, five, and six year olds formed gangs to beg or steal and slept under bridges or in doorways.

Perhaps the parents of these children left the countryside to find work in the city, only to discover that the rumors of jobs and success that come back to the villages are unfounded.

The disappointed family then puts up a cardboard hut, adding on to one of the *favelas* (slums) on a vacant lot or an old garbage dump. The father looks for work, the mother tries to take in washing. The parents hope to exchange cardboard for wood pieces and make the house more permanent. If they hold onto their hut for twenty years, they can own this bit of land.

Finally, the father goes to work in the sugarcane fields or walks 2,000 miles to the industrialized South. In either case he'll be gone for months or years. The sugarcane work is hard. One 1974 study estimated that the people in the sugarcane belt of Pernambuco can expect to live only to age 30.[1]

With the father gone, the mother does her best. Soon a boyfriends's gifts help but new babies are born. So the six year old wanders away. Either s/he can't find home again or learns that the streets yield some reward, as long as one doesn't get caught.

Why do people leave the interior for the cities, we wondered? In some cases, the small land the family owns has been bought by larger landholders, or been lost due to crop failure. Maybe a young man starts a family but there's no place on the parents' five acres for him. Maybe the hope of better conditions, electricity, or job opportunities lures him away. Too often, not gold but *favelas* wait at the end of Rainbow Road.

That's why, we were told, a lot of energy is spent on improving conditions in the interior. Seeds help to replant during crop failures. Wells and cisterns allow survival during droughts. Health clinics mean simple illness isn't usually fatal anymore.

We were anxious, therefore, to visit the villages where our funds had been able to be of use.

Scenes from the interior

We walked down one hill and up another. What a leisure culture we come from. Here, even the simplest tasks — getting water or fuel for the day, working the land, visiting people — absorb a surprising amount of time and energy. We were no longer embarrassed about our red faces, hard breathing, and the sweat that rolled down our cheeks. The goal was not to slip down the steep hill. Bare feet would have fit easier than boots into the toeholds, but bare feet would also have made us vulnerable to parasites.

One hundred miles to the west there is still a desert between us and the Amazon jungle. Here, so close to the coast, plants still grow quickly. Palm and banana trees, and other plants it was hard to guess about, crowded the earth. Farmers hack out a half acre on a hillside and plant rows up and down the hill. The Mennonite missionaries, our hosts in this area, said they have tried to convince people to terrace across the slopes, but because it is so hard to work on the steep hills, few farmers adopt the new method.

We walked through an overgrown area and came upon a spring of fresh water. Most ponds have parasites and snails in them, but this was a spring. The Brazilian guide pointed to a pipe running from the spring. We followed it for a few hundred yards to a cistern our funds had helped to build.

There we met a whitehaired, wrinkled gentleman. He owns the surrounding five acres. It's not clear where this gentleman gets his money – probably under $100/year. Maybe he sells bananas or coconuts to others, or grows a crop for sale. He did say this year's crops were good while last year it was very bad.

His house had a porch and we gladly sat down in its shade. What we would have given for a cool glass of water. But we had been warned not to drink water except as hot coffee for fear of intestinal bugs. We must have looked like we needed something to drink as the gentleman offered to get us some coconuts.

The young Brazilian guide climbed a tree, whacked the coconuts off with the all-purpose machete (big knife) and tossed them below. His forearm was skinned by the time he climbed down. Then the old man took each large green fruit (this stage comes before the hard brown coconuts we see in the stores) and with a sure movement, he whacked the top off, leaving a small hole for us to put to our mouths. We each held a huge green globe to our mouths with both hands and drank the water (not milk — that comes in aged coconuts). It tasted slightly sweet and cool, and we felt refreshed.

★ ★ ★

At the top of the hill was a community center. No teacher comes to the community anymore. Those children that do go to school walk four miles one-way. Many children cannot go because they must help in the family's field. That day there was a weekly health class. The ladies came, dressed in clean cotton. Laundry is done by hand, often on rocks, and may take one or more days a week. Bleach and sun-drying kill the bacteria in the water.

The ladies laughed and talked and looked shyly at the strangers. The lesson was on dehydration in babies. Probably none of these ladies had been out of the village. It is hard to guess how old they were — they all seemed ageless, not quite young on the way to being very old.

It was strange to look at the ladies, knowing that of 35 families in this area, close to half of them have experienced the death of four or more children. Probably most died of easily preventable diseases — diarrhea, measles, or intestinal infections. When Diaconia first came to this area, a staff person asked the men of the village what kind of help they would like. The men talked it over and came back with one request — "please help our children to stop dying." That is how the sanitation projects began.

As the Mennonite missionary explained that the baby's soft spot sinks in when the baby is dehydrated, one lady commented, "Oh that happened to my baby in the morning and it was dead at night." The other ladies nodded.

★ ★ ★

One night we ate at a wooden table by the light of kerosene lamps, which were actually empty vegetable cans topped with a funnel and a kerosene soaked wick burning with an open flame. It certainly got dark with no electricity. Our hostess carried a lamp into another room. Even so, she must have known her way in the dark because the lamp did not light more than three feet from her.

We split a huge plate of potatoes with some margarine on them. Our hostess explained that she serves her guests whatever she is eating. After working all day in the fields, a plate of potatoes is what her family has.

Then it was time to go to the Rosary service, held every night in October. At various homes, people gathered to read the Bible, to reflect on what it meant for their lives and to say the Rosary. The priest was only able to visit the *sitio* (village) once a month. Lay leaders were responsible for the service the rest of the time. People came from miles away, up and down the hilly foot paths. After endless minutes on a dark path, a house appeared, light streaming from the windows.

We entered an 8 foot by 10 foot room. At one end, a picture of Jesus was surrounded by 20 candles. Benches and chairs lined the walls. Brazilian hospitality dictated that the visitors had chairs while others stood. The young men gathered to our right while the young women stood in the middle of the room with their backs to them and us. Older people sat or stood in every other foot of space. Many stood on the porch and looked in the windows. We each took a child on our laps. How slight they seemed for seven or six or eight years old. One pretty, shy little girl looked up with a smile, her eyes permanently crossed.

The service began with a reading from the Portuguese Good News for Modern Man. The passage was the Sermon on the Mount, Matthew 6. The Rosary said, some verses were read again.

"What does this mean for us?" the leader, Antonio, asked. Several people made comments. Then Antonio went on.

"It seems that if people with money were to give it to people without money, the world would believe in Jesus, becasue only the Holy Spirit could accomplish that. Those of us with extra must share with the father who cannot feed his children. Unless we share, that father might think God has not provided for him and be tempted into disbelief. We must safe-guard his faith."

Antonio has ten children and about five acres of land. His face lit up when he talked of God's goodness.

★ ★ ★

At another village we saw more cisterns that our funds had helped to build. Everyone who wanted a cistern got one. Others already had a water source or were afraid that some hidden agenda would mean that their land would be taken once the North American cistern was on their property. So they refused the cistern.

We walked a half mile down a path to see a family breaking stones apart at a pond. The stones would be used in concrete for their cistern. Most of the labor was provided by each family itself. The cisterns would be helpful only if rain came. The hope was that the rainy season, which lasts for several weeks, would fill the cistern for the year.

We asked a local community leader, who organized the cistern project in cooperation with Diaconia and Mennonite Central Committee volunteers, what would be the next step now that most families had access to water and outhouses. "Land" was his quick response.

Three-fourths of the families in areas like this have five or fewer hectares (a hectare is roughly 2.5 acres). Such farms comprise 18 percent of the land and are barely enough for survival. Then 1.1 percent of the farms comprise over a third of the land in plantations of 100 or 1,000 or even 30,000 hectares,[2] often not cultivated by the rich owner, we were told. Land is the issue, called "the social problem" by the rich. Everyone agrees there must be change but no one knows how.

"Can this issue be settled by peaceful change?" we asked. "If there's enough time," was the response, "and the people are patient enough. No one knows: the children are dying today."

Leaving Brazil

The more we got to know the Diaconia staff, the more a feeling of relief developed. How strong is the U.S. pride that we must have all the answers! Clearly, the two of us must have thought to some degree that our task was to go to Brazil and in two weeks straighten out all the problems, returning to Champaign County with a happy report that all is now well. We had to return, instead, with a report that there are some desperate conditions in Brazil that demand our attention. And to think, Brazil is one of the wealthier developing nations. But how happy to be able to report that there are Brazilian Christians who are asking the important questions and developing Brazil's answers. How joyous to recognize that there really is a way to be partners, with some resources available on one side and national insight on the other. We found our enthusiasm for the project growing.

CHAPTER 5
Why Should We Care?

Personal involvement

Both the sewer experience and the trip to Brazil convinced Champaign County Christians of one thing. As one local pastor put it, the poor have faces. John Perkins, Founder and President Emeritus of Voice of Calvary Ministries, Jackson, Mississippi, says it in another way. He asserts that the poor must stop being statistics and start being friends.

Once someone begins to care that there are hurting people in the world, a personal focus seems to be helpful in addressing the need. But why should the Christian start caring in the first place?

Why we should care

As an exercise one can look in a Bible concordance under the heading "poor." First, it is surprising to note that there are a lot of references. Second, some of those references can be disturbing. True, there are those few references which talk about the poor creating their own problems — those are primarily in Proverbs. However, Proverbs says, "He who is kind to the poor, lends to the Lord, and he will repay him for his deed" (Proverbs 19:17) and "He who mocks the poor insults his Maker" (Proverbs 17:5) and

> Give strong drink to him who is perishing, and wine to those in bitter distress; let them drink and forget their poverty, and remember their misery no more. Open your mouth for the dumb, for the rights of all who are left desolate. Open your mouth, judge righteously, maintain the rights of the poor and needy.
> (Proverbs 31:6-9)

There are Old Testament admonitions to care for widows and orphans, dictums to care for the sojourners and the stranger and commands to provide for the needy.

The New Testament also contains many references as to the value of caring for the poor for the sake of justice and righteousness. However, an interesting theme also develops in Jesus' and the writers' teachings.

An element of self-interest

We in *empty tomb* determined early on to give away things in Jesus' name to people who expressed a need for them. We were not, however, always happy about that. There were some people whom it was a pleasure to serve. There were others whom we would rather have shown to the door. Always in this struggle, Luke 6:32–36 was a troubling passage — why did Jesus have to say such things? "Love your enemies, and do good, and lend, expecting nothing in return . . . and you will be sons of the Most High; for he is kind to the ungrateful and the selfish. Be merciful, even as your Father is merciful."

No good going to another translation to look for loopholes as to who qualifies: King James reads "for he is kind unto the unthankful and to the evil." The New International Version labels them "the ungrateful and the wicked." Even if we are to love the nice poor, does God actually mean the ungrateful qualify too?

Finally, a light dawned. Jesus' comments were not addressed to the unthankful and the wicked but to the person who would be Jesus' follower. It is not the follower's job to judge the other person's condition, but only to be faithful him- or herself to the commands of God. The person expressing need is not required to make a profession of faith. The person seeking to serve Jesus has made such a profession. Jesus tells his follower, do this — then your reward will be great and you will be sons of the Most High.

This theme is continued in Luke 6:46 when Jesus says, "So why do you call me 'Lord' when you won't obey me?" (Living Bible) and the more encouraging, "And be sure to put into practice what you hear. The more you do this, the more you will understand what I tell you" (Mark 4:24 LB). In Matthew 25:31–46, Jesus raises the question as to whether someone claiming to be his follower knows him if s/he is not seeking out opportunities to feed, clothe, and visit the oppressed. This thought is echoed in James 2 and 1 John 3:16-18. Apparently, if we want to grow in our knowledge of God, we will do what Jesus tells us: serve others. So one can conclude that as we care about the poor, we will also grow with Jesus.

A personal concern

The command is to love our neighbor as ourselves. One of our co-workers had an interesting insight into the parable of the Good Samaritan (Luke 10:36). By the end of the story Jesus has turned the initial question around from "Who is my neighbor?" into the provocative question, to whom are you willing to be a neighbor?

It is convenient to move to a nice neighborhood and attend a homogeneous church. Our neighbors may irritate us or get on our nerves, but generally they smell okay (or don't smell at all) and don't threaten us either emotionally or physically. However, if Jesus commands us to love the poor, perhaps Christians who are otherwise isolated from the poor should seek out opportunities to be with them. The way our society is now set up, it is entirely possible never to meet a poor person. The concerned Christian, then, may have to make a special effort to seek out those whom s/he can serve. This idea has surfaced in mission outreaches all over the United States.

PART II

PART II

The desire to be faithful to Jesus' commands must be translated into action if it is to benefit anyone on a practical level. The strategies offered here are formed by the commitment to the value of personal involvement and the awareness of the great income possessed by church members in the U.S.A.

On a domestic level, the strategy of Christian Family to Family Relationships is offered as a practical concept for approaching need within the U.S. in Chapter 6.

The idea of such relationships, although not widely implemented, is not a totally new one. For example, the LaSalle Street Church in Chicago is actively trying to involve its own church members and suburban church members in relationships with residents of a neighboring low-income housing project. The National Presbyterian Church in Washington, D.C., cooperates with an inner-city congregation on work projects and fellowship, with an eye toward developing friendships. One Ministries, Inc., also in Washington, is attempting to match a suburban church with an inner-city church so together they can address the needs of a particular city block. In cities throughout the country, the benefit to both parties in personal relationships between a better-off Christian and a poorer Christian or non-Christian is emphasized.

In our own experience we have felt that such personal relationships are important in bridging the gaps that allow poverty to exist alongside such great wealth in the U.S.

Chapters 7 and 8 explore missions on an international level. The world scene is rapidly changing in regard to governments, resources, and communications. The brief overview of missions in Chapter 7 points to the need for a coordinated and comprehensive approach to the world mission task.

A strategy to respond to this need is suggested in Chapter 8. Each county in the U.S. is matched with an area of evangelism and/or physical need in the world. Based on potential resources and number of adherents within the U.S. church, this matching suggests that it is possible to break down "world poverty" into approachable segments. This matching project is called Yoking.

Again, the concept of such matching is not completely new. The need for more personal focus has been effectively translated into the various child-sponsorship programs which are operated by both denominational and interdenominational organizations. The sponsor is able to understand that s/he is making a significant difference in the life of one child.

The Roman Catholic Church has encouraged the concept of twinning: one U.S. Parish Conference "twins" with a particular Parish Conference in the developing world for mission projects. The Southern Baptist Convention has a similar emphasis between churches in Texas and Brazil. Individual congregations of various denominations have selected particular areas or missionaries in the world for special concern.

The contribution of the yoking strategy is the comprehensive way in which each U.S. county, given its adherent Christian population and potential resources, is matched with a specific area of the world.

Both the domestic and international strategies depend heavily on the "potential resources of the church in the U.S." What are these resources? And who says they exist? In Chapter 9, the scene is set for this discussion by exploring the idea of "applying the fruits of production." It is in Chapter 10 that statistics and tables are offered that suggest Christians in the U.S. possess hidden billions of dollars that could be applied to the task of proclaiming and acting on the Gospel of Jesus Christ.

CHAPTER 6

Christian Family to Family Relationships

Getting to know you

In 1 John 4:20, the apostle points out that one cannot hate his brother whom he has seen and still say he can love God, whom he has not seen. In the same vein, Christians may have a warm heart for world mission but the concern rings hollow unless local action is also pursued. How can the Christian be concerned about those in need whom s/he hasn't seen overseas and yet not be concerned about the need in his or her own town?

There is much to be learned about reaching out to the poor who are close at hand. John Perkins notes that outreach to the local poor "grinds up fictitiousness." One may start out sharing with the poor, confident of one's own generous nature. Soon, however, the inconvenience of sharing drives the concerned Christian to his or her knees. To continue to go against one's own self-interest requires a growing dependence on God's Spirit. This lesson is very important if U.S. Christians are going to be serious about meeting the needs of those in other countries, with even greater needs.

Second, one can experience "culture shock" while still in the safe environs of one's own community. Growing in appreciation for different cultures requires that the Christian's concept of God grows, too. It is too easy to make God in our image. By getting to know Christians across town who are of a different culture, either because of economics, race and/or ethnicity, the Christian can begin to separate real Christian conviction from societal conditioning.

This process also allows for the U.S. Christian to identify more with the world population. Also, our brothers and sisters in Christ who are missionaries in foreign lands face similar culture shocks. To the degree that those of us who stay at home are growing cross-culturally, we can truly identify better with the missionary's struggles, and provide better support, both in prayer and correspondence.

Oneness in Christ's body

Finally, there is real value in reaching out cross-culturally in our own town because Jesus prays that his followers would be one (John 17). There is a present school of thought that the local congregations should be a homogeneous unit, that is, everyone similar to everyone else. There is strong thought that congregations should be communities in which everyone is like everyone else because people " . . . like to become Christians without crossing racial, linguistic or class barriers." When this option is not available, "people reject the gospel not because they think it is false, but because it strikes them as alien."[1]

There may be real insight in this church growth model. Once in the kingdom, however, it is too easy to mistake the homogeneous unit as the complete body of Christ — everyone who is truly a Christian is just like us. The old standard story of the tour group in Heaven illustrates the point. As St. Peter showed the group around, they came to one doorway. St. Peter motioned for everyone to be quiet and tiptoe past the door. A safe distance away, one person asked the purpose of the exercise. "Oh," replies St. Peter, "that's the room for (insert denomination) — they think they're the only ones here."

Or consider this experience. Once we went to a service in the basement of a little church. An elderly black woman was preaching. We were the only whites in the small audience. Suddenly she stopped her sermon and pointed a finger at us as her eyes glistened. "God loves us all," she exclaimed. "I ain't goin' to Heaven wifout yo'," she went on, "but yo sho' ain't goin' wifout me, neider."

As a good friend of ours repeats, the ground at the foot of the cross is level. We fool ourselves if any group of us thinks we don't need other Christians. Paul points out in 1 Corinthians 12 that different gifts are given to different members of the church so that together we can make a whole body. Ephesians 4 notes that different gifts and talents in the church are given " . . . for building up the body of Christ, until we all attain to the unity of the faith and of the knowledge of the Son of God, to mature manhood, to the measure of the stature of the fulness of Christ . . . " (Ephesians 4:12, 13).

If we get to know the poor across town and they are not Christian, then we have the opportunity to combine actions with our words in our testimony of God's love for them, proclaiming Jesus' good news to them. In many cases, though, the poor are in fact Christians, and then we can build up Christ's body.

Commenting on John 17, a writer notes,

"From this passage in John we understand that the most powerful method for evangelism today is the church united in a given locale, working, moving, and sharing together as a community of love. It seems as if we have ignored this vital statement of Jesus concerning the world believing in Jesus when the church gets united. We have tried every gimmick and procedure imaginable to the ingenuity of man when God's method for reaching a city is a united church."[2]

The practical implications of U.S. Christians reaching out to Christians different from themselves should also be evident when one considers that as of the mid-1970's Christians in Third World countries outnumbered Western Christians.[3]

We U.S. Christians do not have a corner on Jesus. We must therefore get to know him as he is revealing himself throughout the world, including across town.

How to begin

There may already be Christian outreaches in your congregation or community which provide opportunities for the individual to reach out cross-culturally in Jesus' name. One can go to the pastor, the social concerns committee of the church or an interdenominational outreach in your city. Such outreaches, often focusing on making contact with the poor person, may already exist for you or your congregation to join.

The ministries through *empty tomb* have focused on such personal contact. We do not define our work as an outreach to the poor, but rather as a challenge to the church. The Bible lays the responsibility of the poor on the church, not some sub-set of the church. The task then is to provide ways for the church to act on that responsibility.

Discipleship opportunities

The staff members at *empty tomb* view themselves as provid-ing discipleship opportunities for Christians and congregations. Sorting clothes and delivering furniture, sharing food, sharing in a Bible Study, helping with home repair are all offered as volunteer opportunities. Time commitment varies from an isolated hour to a regular schedule, always under supervision.

In addition, on the second Saturday of each month, we have a Christian Family to Family Dinner. Christians from different congregations, racial and economic backgrounds gather for a potluck. After dinner an offering is taken, each person is asked to put in according to ability, but at least a penny. Next, the baskets are passed again, each person is encouraged to take out according to need, but everyone should take at least a penny. Any money left over is put into the next month's offering. A short lesson and discussion or a brief program follows. In this way, Christians who might not otherwise meet are offered an opportunity for fellowship on a neutral ground.

Christian family to family relationships

We have been learning from these outreaches. Our hope that friendships would develop from such contacts through the sharing or the monthly dinners has been well-founded in some cases. More often than not, however, the contacts help to break down stereotypes but do not grow into real friendship.

So we've been trying to develop a Christian Family to Family Relationships work. We envision a covenant, signed by two families. A specific goal would be set, such as a child being tutored to pass seventh grade. Expectations on both sides would be clear. The well-to-do Christians might agree to tutor the child three afternoons a week. The child's parent(s) would agree to have the child at home at the specified time, and make sure the child does assignments. In addition, the families would agree to come to the Dinners together. Support from their pastors and perhaps even an experienced staff person would be available to help interpret one family to the other.

This idea sounds pretty structured, doesn't it? How can a friendship grow up with so much intentional organization? However, with all the fears and prejudices, with the lack of progress being made in such cross-cultural friendships we ask instead, how can we grow together without such structure?

Questions arise

Thinking on reaching out, we find the issue complicated as relationships develop. For example:

1. How can realistic expectations be communicated? How does one prepare the financially better-off Christian for the fact that lack of money is not the only reason people are poor? How can the poor person understand that the better-off person does not have endless resources?

2. How does one determine that individuals on both sides have the commitment to see the relationship through? The better-off Christian probably has money options which are not available to the poor person. How can one be sure the better-off person won't get bored or frightened and suddenly feel "a different calling," leaving the poor person now not only poor but also rejected?

3. How does a couple reach out to a family headed by a single mother, safeguarding against any jealousy or confusion which might result?

4. How is the dignity of both participants safeguarded in such a sharing situation? Could the poor person end up doing "favors" for the better-off Christian, such as house cleaning, in return for such sharing, and instead end up just an underpaid maid?

Start simply

It is not that we have been lazy or slow these last eleven years as we have tried to grow toward encouraging deeper relationships among people who are different. Rather, the issues that keep people separated in society are very real, and require a lot of thought as well as action.

Perhaps the best approach is to begin slowly. The richer Christian should first study the Bible and be convinced in his or her heart that such an outreach is important. Then the Christian should volunteer to be in available cross-cultural settings. The Christian thus reaching out should talk about the struggles and joys of this outreach with others doing similar activities. Perhaps a Sunday school class or a Bible Study would want to take on a monthly food delivery program as a group. Finally, the Christian should not lose sight of the fact that it is for love of God, which wells over into love for neighbor, that the Christian steps out in faith. If you are not already reaching out in this way, it may surprise you how much joy God has in store for you.

In any case, the Christian who is loving the local neighbor likely has an increased appetite to love the overseas neighbor, where the need is even greater.

CHAPTER 7
Missions in the 1980's

Changing times

Missions, whether emphasizing word or deed, must adapt to the circumstances of the people being contacted. In recent years, many changes have taken place. As mission agencies strive to adapt, many times the missionary finds himself struggling to learn about the new environment and also interpret it to supporters back home. One agency describes the plight of the Western agency as being " . . . stretched between two poles." The agency needs to interpret the mission situation to its supporters, taking into account those supporters' pictures of the world. At the same time, the agency needs to interact with the " . . . churches through whom and with whom it attempts to work in the Third World . . . " This tension exists whether the task is evangelism or country development.[1]

And this dilemma faces denominational as well as interdenominational mission agencies; Roman Catholic orders as well as Protestant mission boards.

Growth of nationalism

The U.S. Christian at home might wonder if missionaries are even welcome in Third World countries any more. There seems to be an emphasis on each country's church developing its own identity. Words such as "liberation" and "base communities" have strange sounds which arouse fears of political confusion. The mission agency must also come to terms with this nationalism and interpret this trend to the Christian in the American pew.

Harvey T. Hoekstra states that "The end of colonialism and the entry of nations into international institutions was to have a profound effect upon the missionary movement . . . " He notes that some countries closed their doors to missions while others took over formerly mission-run schools and hospitals. With independence came the growing sense of mutuality in mission. He points out, for example, " . . . appropriate structures, patterns of relationships, ownership of property and program, access to funds and independence of their use . . . the search for patterns of partnership, how mission was to be understood . . . ", all these topics now were open to debate.[2]

The mission agencies continue to come to terms with these changing circumstances. Often, part of the difficulty in explaining the mission outreach to the supporters in the U.S. is having only broad, general categories in which to fit the experience on a particular mission field. Yet changes in the perception of the U.S. church must come if the U.S. church is to continue to play a vital role in the world church.

For example, churches in Third World countries have been taking increased initiative and claiming greater responsibility for mission efforts in their own areas. There is increased clarity among mission agencies regarding the need for Christians in the U.S. to fit in with, cooperate more fully with, and learn from the leadership of Christians in Third World countries. Some leaders even see a shift in the center of Christianity. Walbert Bühlmann, General Secretary for Missionary Animation of the Franciscan-Capuchin Secretariat in Rome, suggests that the center of Christianity has shifted from the West to the Southern Hemisphere. It is here, in Latin America, Africa, Asia-Oceania, that in the third millennium the "major inspiration to the worldwide church will originate."[3]

If such a shift is taking place, ways must be found to communicate this reality to the U.S. Christian.

Chaos and confusion

The growth in nationalism ended the idea of comity as well. Comity was the arrangement whereby major world powers divided up the developing world into spheres of influence: e.g., the Belgian Congo, French Equitorial Africa, the English in India. It was the responsibility of the church in the controlling nation to evangelize the people under the influence of that government.

One cannot picture a return to such a comity relationship between nations in the developed and developing world. The nationalism among developing countries is a generally healthy trend for the church.

But the international mission movement still seems to be floundering for a strategy to replace comity. Emilio Castro notes that comity lent a certain order to the mission enterprise in the past. "Today an almost total chaos prevails." The result is that " . . . fifty different versions of the gospel are being sent from North America all over the world . . . " which causes trouble for the local national churches and only amuses " . . . the secular or religious societies that observe this garbled witness."[4]

This lack of cooperation can not only provide a confusing witness, but can have negative instead of positive consequences for the people on the receiving end. The Christian in the U.S. supporting missions often legitimately wants to know whether the assistance provided is being used wisely. It appears that in some instances there is need for more coordination among church agencies for the gifts to be used in the best possible way.

For example, the United Nations World Food Council published a paper entitled "The African Food Problem and the Role of International Agencies." The problems resulting from lack of agency coordination that the report cites ranged from ineffectiveness in aid distribution to actually threatening the stability of the government aid programs. Among other points made, the report stated that 1) "The coordination problems faced by African countries in dealing with large numbers of agencies, each with its own special preference for sectors and forms of assistance needs to be more fully understood;" 2) Each recipient country should be encouraged to coordinate all foreign assistance as that country applies the assistance to its own programs; and 3) It should be clear that countries with weak administrations can actually be destabilized by aid received if such aid is not appropriately coordinated. The report notes that in one country where 340 assistance missions were active " . . . the government was not always able to keep up with the management and coordination requirements, with resulting confusion at all levels and a loss of resources and efficiency . . . "[5]

It would be unfair to say, nor are we implying, that much of the good work currently being accomplished through church mission agencies is lost due to lack of coordination with other agencies. Nor are we saying there is currently no cooperation among agencies. Nevertheless, there appears to be a role for developing an overall strategy in missions which eliminates duplication of efforts and mission outreaches working at cross-purposes. If Christians in the U.S. are to be challenged to greater mission commitment, we need assurance that this increased aid can be put to effective use.

Understanding the need

If it is difficult for a concerned Christian to understand the struggles and circumstances facing her poor neighbor across town, it is also difficult for the Christian to understand the life situation of the neighbor overseas.

For example, consider the topic of Gross National Product (GNP). The per capita GNP in a country may appear to be pretty high. If the average person in Brazil has $2050 according to the 1980 GNP, the average Brazilian should be doing okay.

It is not, however, that simple. Robert S. McNamara, former President of the World Bank Group, noted that in many countries " . . . there has been a serious neglect of equity in the distribution of employment opportunities, and in the allocation of public services that effect productivity." As a result, he asserts, income distribution is "severely skewed." He goes on to say that this pattern cannot be attributed, on the whole, to a temporary growth pattern. Rather, the benefits that have come with increased gross national products have " . . . accrued disproportionately to the already more favored income groups in their societies, and broadened rather than narrowed the gap between the privileged and the deprived." He concludes that social unrest has been a result of this unfair distribution of economic growth benefits and suggests that new institutional and policy frameworks must be developed to prevent more unrest.[6]

Shavid Javed Burki, a Pakistani who served as the Chief of the Policy Planning Division in the Policy Planning and Program Review Department of the World Bank, also notes the dynamic of distribution has as great an importance as availability of resources. He asserts that there is enough food to supply everyone with 3,000 calories a day. Rather, the problem " . . . is one of distribution between countries, regions, and income groups and within households."[7]

Shavid Javed Burki then proceeds to point out the conflict between various constituencies or people groups. He notes that powerful groups within countries can make distribution of food and necessary resources very difficult. "There are a number of instances of powerful constituencies blocking the transfer of public financial and administrative resources from secondary and university education to primary education, from urban to rural health, from high-cost curative health facilities to relatively low-cost preventive care."[8]

Lester Brown and Gail Finsterbusch explore this point in a discussion of conflicts that arise in the distribution of new agricultural technologies. They note that often landowners and tenants are at odds with each other or with landless laborers, and that the landless even may argue among themselves. They recount how forty-two persons were burned to death in December, 1968 in one Indian village in an argument among landless laborers. The landowners were using new technology. Fighting over the best way to gain a share of the expected increase in benefits from this technology, one group of landless laborers wanted to boycott the landowners until wages were raised while the other group was willing to work at current rates.[9]

Francis Moore Lappé and Joseph Collins emphasize this point, that when working on development one must understand the impact of a project and the circumstances of the people being assisted. The reality is that people within an area often work against each other. An anthropologist working in Bangladesh told Lappé and Collins " . . . that the fundamental social reality is a struggle over land: the well-off do everything possible to get their smaller neighbors in debt to them in order to foreclose on their land; the poor farmers do everything possible to hold onto the little land they have, even hiring out wives and daughters for demeaning servant's work . . ."10

Interpreting the need

The task of the missionary and mission agency becomes a complicated one. The missionary must understand the culture in which s/he hopes to introduce the verbal Gospel. The missionary very often must address the desperate physical conditions of the people around him/her, and understand the impact of that aid on the local economy and power structures while coordinating this aid with the national church, the government and other entities. In addition, the missionary must understand his/her role as a servant in the national church. Part of this role may include helping to provide a forum back in the U.S. for national church leaders, so that U.S. Christians may learn from overseas Christians. And if the Christian at home in America is to be made a vital partner in this venture, all of this reality must be interpreted to those back in the U.S. so that they can grow in understanding. It helps if the Christians back home are seeking out local cross-cultural experiences to help them identify with a different people. Yet the interpretation task is still tremendous.

We should thank God for those faithful followers of his who are willing to step out on the front lines and face these overwhelming realities. They are valiant men and women from the U.S. as well as many other nations who join missionary orders, apply to mission boards or struggle to coordinate this very important task of the body of Christ worldwide.

But we owe them something more. Perhaps those of us who do not enlist firsthand to go to the mission field should struggle to become as knowledgeable about missions as possible.

Christians do not have to wait to have international reality interpreted for them. Perhaps the Christian can seek out educational opportunities.

It would be helpful to have an overall strategy for the concerned Christian to fit into. It is impossible for anyone to understand the whole world's need, the cultures, the possibilities. To allow for the coordination for which experts express a need, to encourage in-depth understanding of people in need in a particular country or area, to allow the individual Christian to educate himself, we have developed a strategy. We call it a Yoking Map.

CHAPTER 8
A Yoking Map

Area to area

The personal emphasis which developed in our local work has value in the international realm as well. If U.S. Christians are to be concerned about the overseas neighbor, it helps to have specifics and feedback. In the international mission effort, too, we must strive to make the poor friends instead of statistics.

One way of accomplishing this task is by matching one area of the U.S. with an area overseas. As mentioned earlier, the Southern Baptists, the Roman Catholics and other denominations have explored this idea already. One value of such matching is that a partnership can develop on both sides of the arrangement. Christians in the U.S. with resources to share can also communicate experiences, insight and knowledge which may be of use in the mission context. On the other hand, the U.S. Christian has the opportunity to know one area of the world in more depth. Why do people lose land? What is the greatest need — seeds, water, land, Bibles? What Gospel insights do Christians in developing rural areas have which might challenge and refresh the U.S. Christian? Long-term commitment can beget friendship, with all its lovely fruits.

Partnership

The idea of partnership may be a strategy which allows for order and depth in mission work. Mission agencies would not have to plead for money as each new crisis arrives: a group of U.S. Christians would already be committed to the area. If an unusual crisis arose, missions in surrounding areas could choose to forward some of the money being received from U.S. sources. Resources could be more evenly distributed and feedback is more possible.

The idea of partnership has been recommended by Hugo Zorilla, a Mennonite Brethren Church leader from Columbia who has served as Dean of the Latin America Biblical Seminary, San Jose, Costa Rica. He asserts, "So today in the missionary task, a fraternal relationship between churches of different regions should have a primacy in mission thinking . . . and thereby generate mutual edification, interchange of personnel for specific tasks, and economic cooperation."[1]

Growing together

It is not to say that such partnership or area to area commitment eliminates the awkward parts of mission outreach or solves all the problems. However, narrowing world need from the whole planet to a specific area can allow communication to begin and a sharing to develop which allows for mutual dignity.

For example, the United Presbyterian Church has taken an interest in the concept of partnering. In an article in which he described the good that had come out of the financial sharing which had taken place, Frederick R. Wilson, Associate General Director for Ecumenical and Interchurch Relations for the Program Agency of the United Presbyterian Church, reflected on developing a partnership with an area overseas. He notes that it is difficult to develop such reciprocal relationships in mission when one group has money to share and the other has a need. Even the responsible act of wanting to be accountable to donors " . . . makes us appear to be seeking to control expenditures when our declared intention is to make a gift." Instead of joining in a conversation about " . . . what God is calling the church in India to do . . . " the situation develops into " . . . negotiation as we seek to agree on the terms of a financial transaction."

> " . . . With other Christians we need to create something to function as an altar on which we, and those with whom we serve, may place our gifts. Then we can 'empty our hands.' This is a priority task for the 80's. It cannot be done swiftly or easily. Our creativity, our flexibility, our patience and our efforts to understand one another will be taxed to the limit."[2]

But it may be that the very reality of this exploration process will involve U.S. Christians in a way not now possible. Missions become not an abstract duty but a relationship to be developed, prayed through and struggled with.

A Yoking Map

Each of us has probably been involved in a meal when the comment was made, "Finish your food — there are children starving in India who would love to have it." The standard rebellious response to this phrase is, "Then send it to them."

Imagine the difference in conversation, however, if the parent were to say, "Eat your food — Jimmy across the street is going to starve because he doesn't have it." The response might not be rebellious, but sincere: "Can't I eat less and share some with Jimmy?"

It is precisely this type of personalizing that yoking hopes to accomplish. The poor children of India may still be the focus at a dinner table in Atlanta, Georgia, but parents in Corpus Christi, Texas could comment on the plight of children in a particular Latin American country and a parent in Boston, Massachusetts could reflect on the children in a specific African nation. The goal of yoking is to remove the need of the world from the "them out there" concept to "our friends in this area," to remind us that indeed, the poor do have faces.

To encourage an orderly yoking process, a Yoking Map has been developed. A first step in developing the map was to determine the level of resources each country required for both its evangelism and material needs. Needing a figure at which to consider a country "evangelized," the number of Christians in each country was listed. Those countries in which 50 percent or more of the population is Christian were considered to be in a position to reach the non-Christians in their own country. Those nations with a Christian population less than 50 percent were assigned resources to assist in evangelizing the non-Christians there. Each country which is 0–49 percent Christian was assigned a certain Evangelism Need Number based on the percentage of Christians in that country.

Next, each country was listed with its Gross National Product (GNP). The GNP is a fairly good indicator of where a country stands in relationship to other countries. The GNP, however, does not indicate how well the country's income is spread around *within* that particular country. Nevertheless, the GNP provides an available comparative worldwide scale of economic conditions. Each country with less than the world's average GNP was assigned a Development Need Number, depending on how much below the average it was.

The Evangelism Need Number and the Development Need Number were then combined on a 1:10 ratio to determine the Need Index for that country. Assigning ten times the resources to development than to evangelism does not mean that development is seen as the more important of the two. This weighting process merely reflects the practical problem that the cost of development projects often is greater than the actual cost of evangelism projects. Even so, it is estimated that this allocation allows for a 500 percent increase over current word missions.[3]

Knowing the amount of need of each country, the next step was to determine how much money U.S. Christians have to share. This figure was obtained by finding out how many church adherents live in each U.S. county and how much total personal income people in that county receive. Figuring a percentage of people's income for overseas missions, an actual figure can be determined that is available, in theory, to share with people in evangelism and physical needs overseas. One assumption should be noted here. It is our opinion that the U.S. church should be doing a great deal more in the area of missions and financial sharing. It is hoped that the Yoking Map will make missions enough of a challenge to actually increase mission giving. Further discussion on this topic is contained in a following chapter.

Geographic matching

In matching the U.S. counties with a nation in need, geographic lines were kept in mind. The west coast of the U.S. was assigned to the countries across the Pacific from them. The east coast was matched with Africa. The south central area was yoked with Latin America. There were at least two reasons for trying to keep some geographical order in the Yoking Map.

First, Christians in a particular county may want to visit the mission area with which they are yoked. Clearly, India is on the opposite side of the world from the U.S. and would be a long distance from any county. But the west coast is closest to eastern Asia, and the east coast is closer to Africa. Some visiting efforts may be a little more convenient by virtue of this assignment.

The other reason to match areas geographically is to help mission education here in the United States. The northeast could have a conference on Africa and Christians could gather together from a several state area at a central place. The same is true for Christians wanting to gather to consider outreach in Latin America or the Middle East or the Far East.

Christians wanting to have a conference on China in the U.S. would likely have a far way to go and this fact is interesting in itself. If you refer to the Yoking Map 1: The United States, you can count how many entire states are matched with Asia excluding the Middle East: 39! One may say that some of the states out west that are assigned to China are the less populated states: Wyoming, Montana, South Dakota. But also such states as Illinois and Michigan, with large population centers, are matched with China. The map is a concrete visual presentation of the large evangelism and development need in Asia which challenges U.S. Christians.

Another look at the Yoking Map 1: The United States provides an additional insight into the great resources of U.S. Christians. If Christians in this country were seriously to share some of our abundance, it appears we could accomplish a great deal. The Evangelism and Need Numbers of Africa are high. Nevertheless, according to our figures, there are enough financial resources in the northeast states of Maine, Vermont, New Hampshire, Connecticut, Massachusetts and part of the state of New York for Christians to address many of those needs! Consider the resources in Texas. If Christians in that state were seriously to act on Jesus' commandment to love our neighbor, Christians in Texas alone could band together with their Latin American brothers and sisters in Christ to address those important needs.

Following are the Yoking Maps. The first, of the United States, shows the names of the country or countries with which each state is matched. For a listing by U.S. county with a specific country, see Appendix A.

The second map, Yoking Map 2: The World, shows the countries and lists the states' abbreviations with which they are matched. For a reference list by country, showing the states matched with it, refer to Appendix B.

Individual use of the Yoking Map

By referring to Appendix A, a Christian in any county in the United States can find out the name of a nation with which s/he is matched. The U.S. Christian can begin to look into what the conditions and needs are in that country and what Christians there are doing about the situation. A cross-reference Appendix also allows the reader to look up a specific country and see with which state(s) it is matched.

The use of the Appendices could be important for a Christian concerned about world need. Too often, an individual who wants to respond to Christ's command and reach out in Jesus' name can be stopped cold — where to begin? How does one get a congregation to become more concerned? How can someone understand what the real situation is?

A Christian using the Yoking Map has at least a next step to pursue. Finding that the county in which one lives is matched with a specific nation, one can write one's denominational or interdenominational headquarters for more information. Are there missionaries already there? Is there a national church in the area? What are the needs perceived to be? How long do people live? What is the average per capita income? How can Christians in the U.S. contribute to help people there? Immediately the Christian can make the area a matter for prayer.

Another focus for the interested Christian which results from the Yoking Map is the amount of money conceivably available for missions from U.S. Christians (see Table A, Chapter 10). The Christian concerned about missions has, from the Table, a suggested schedule of giving. Comparing the giving level of one's own congregation, the concerned Christian can undertake education, fund-raising and prayer projects to address the specific needs of the area to which s/he is yoked. Such activity may soon lead one to a seat on the congregation's mission committee!

Area use of the Yoking Map

It may be that churches in each U.S. county or area might want to cooperate on a common mission focus. Those congregations could explore oneness in Christ's body in the U.S. while learning to become one with Christians overseas. Two or three congregations of the same denomination or fifty congregations from many denominations might cooperate on such a focus.

The advantages of such cooperation are many. Common educational conferences, visitors from and to the overseas area and distribution of end-use materials would be made easier with shared expenses and coordination. Locally we have found over forty county congregations willing to cooperate on our focus on Brazil.

How is the Yoking Map matching to be built into current mission commitments? Perhaps considering our experience in Champaign County might be helpful. It is interesting to note that Champaign County is matched with China on the Yoking Map. The current focus on Brazil could be reconciled with the yoking suggestion of China in one of several ways. Champaign County Christians could, for example, make contacts with Texas Christians, who are matched on the Yoking Map with Brazil, and over a period of years, shift the current projects and contacts in Brazil to Texas. Since the Yoking Map is designed to encourage additional mission giving, over and above current efforts, the Brazil project could be maintained as a "current project," and an additional focus on China could be fostered.

Such continuing contacts with Brazil would have to be handled with a sensitivity to any increasing activity in Brazil by Texas Christians. Champaign County Christians might want to be open to a complete shift to China as they develop relationships with Christians in China, and as the benefits of efficient mission fund distribution become evident. In any case, the deciding factor will be whether Christians want to be obedient to Jesus' commands to reach out in his name. If they do, then there will be enough commitment to work out the specifics.

Our cooperative fund-raising efforts have resulted in local secular publicity about the good the church of Jesus Christ is able to accomplish. Getting teams from 25 churches together to build a house in a day for a local family in need while raising over $12,000 for the Brazil focus was covered by two TV stations and the newspaper. People coming together to discuss how to share time and resources provides a creative setting in which Christians from different backgrounds can work together and thus know each other. Finally, from the feedback we have gotten, it appears that this cooperative effort has attracted new money into missions, increasing total mission giving in our county, rather than taking money away from current denominational mission giving.

Denominational use of the Yoking Map

Each denomination already has overseas mission outreaches designed to allow those Christians to respond to the Great Commission in both word and deed mission. The Yoking Map could be a supplement to those efforts, a further challenge to greater mission efforts. In other cases, the Yoking Map could provide an overall strategy to interpret missions to the denomination's constituents, giving the church members a feeling of more immediate access to the mission outreach of the church.

The denomination could limit support of the Yoking Map to providing the names of missionaries in particular areas to interested individual Christians. The denomination could encourage an increased commitment to missions by challenging members of its denominational congregations to cooperate on a

supplemental missions project, focusing on the particular area
assigned to them.

The Yoking concept, however, could be build into a re-
organization of the mission outreach of the church. The
denomination could take the initiative in providing end-use
from one area of the world to an area in the U.S. Visits of
church leaders in the matched areas could be exchanged.
Educational materials and furlough missionary tours could
be more efficiently developed with the specific area-to-area
arrangement in mind.

The value of a Yoking Map

Matching countries in need with specific areas in the United
States has some value in addition to making the poor more
real to Christians in the U.S.

For one thing, the map encourages an orderly distribution
of U.S. resources and attention throughout the areas of need.
It is easy in this day of mass communication for one crisis to
be highlighted as *the* area in need. The result is that mission
agencies are faced with the task of making each new crisis seem
worse than the previous one. The Christian from whom money
is being requested feels that the world is one hopeless mess with
little progress being made. A certain numbness results from
appeal after appeal.

In yoking, a specific area in need would be the continuing
responsibility of a specific set of Christians. If tragedy were to
strike that area and increased aid were needed, perhaps Christians currently uninvolved in the county could be challenged to
participate. Perhaps funds for development projects could be
diverted to relief. Perhaps the U.S. Christian could even be
challenged to go beyond the current giving level. If a serious
disaster were to happen in a particular country or area, other
states assigned to that continent could channel some of their
resources to the area by mutual agreement. However, each
area of the world would have specific U.S. Christians concerned
about it on an ongoing basis.

Yoking also allows for coordinated efforts on behalf of mission agencies and the Christians supporting them. As has been pointed out, the lack of coordination among mission efforts can have devastating effects on a country. Mission leaders at the national level benefit from having informed and enthusiastic involvement at the local U.S. levels. Interdenominational, denominational and independent agencies and associations will feel challenged to work out coordinated strategies for specific areas of need. Cross-cultural missionaries can visit particular areas of the U.S. and share information with people who are educated about the situation the missionary is facing. Imagine the informed and specific prayers the U.S. Christians can offer on behalf of the area with which they are matched.

In addition to these advantages, yoking encourages a oneness in the body of Christ in the U.S. county or area. Christians, regardless of denomination, have a common focus. Even though a specific group may emphasize word evangelism while another focuses on material need, understanding the area and raising funds to help the area brings U.S. Christians in communication with each other. Creative provisions can be outlined in advance for the distribution of any money raised through joint efforts. Imagine the witness of a citywide mission festival sponsored by all the churches in the area could be.

Yoking can also consider the need for development[4] in largely evangelized areas of the Third World and yet not ignore the need of unreached people where evangelism need is as great as the development need. Since the evangelism and development needs have been taken into consideration, the Third World area is matched with sufficient U.S. counties to help address both these needs.

The major purpose of yoking is to make the challenge of world mission as clear and as exciting as it ought to be to each U.S. Christian. Having great resources, we Christians in the U.S. have not yet risen to the challenge of loving the rest of the world as much as God does. There is a wonderful opportunity awaiting each of us to come to know and understand Christians and non-Christians in another specific part of the world. We will need to educate ourselves to the needs, learn to communicate cross-culturally and be open to growing in understanding of how Christianity is manifested elsewhere in the world. The rewards will be those given to all who seek to be obedient to Jesus' commands. God has promised to provide the ways and means to follow him if only we will try.

YOKING MAP 1: The United States

Afghanistan
Bahrain
Iran
Iraq
Israel
Jordan
Kuwait
Lebanon
Oman
Pakistan
Qatar
Saudi Arabia
Syria
United Arab
  Emirates
Yemen, North
Yemen, South

Benin
Cape Verde
Egypt
Gambia
Ghana
Guinea
Guinea-Bissau
Ivory Coast
Liberia
Mali
Mauritania
Morocco
Niger
Nigeria
Senegal
Sierra Leone
Togo
Upper Volta
Western Sahara

Cameroon
Central African
  Republic
Chad

Angola
Cameroon
Congo
Equatorial Guinea
Sao Tome and Principe
St. Helena

Albania
Portugal
Romania

South
  Africa
Swaziland
Botswana
Lesotho

Angola

Namibia

Burundi
Central African
  Republic
Comoros
Kenya
Madagascar
Malawi
Mauritius
Mayotte
Mozambique
Rwanda
Seychelles
Tanzania
Uganda
Zaire
Zambia
Zimbabwe

Djibouti
Ethiopia
Kenya
Somalia

Algeria
Ethiopia
Libya
Morocco
Sudan
Tunisia

MINN

WIS

MICH

IOWA

ILL

IND

OHIO

PA

NY

VT

NH

MASS

CONN

RI

NJ

MD

DC

DEL

W VA

VA

KY

NC

SC

MO

ARK

TENN

ALA

GA

MISS

LA

FLA

China

China

China

China

China

China

China

China

China

China

Pakistan

India

India

India

India

India

India

India

India

India

India

India

India

India

Turkey

Bhutan

Nepal

Bangladesh

Bangladesh

Maldives

Sri
Lanka

MAINE

YOKING MAP 2: The World

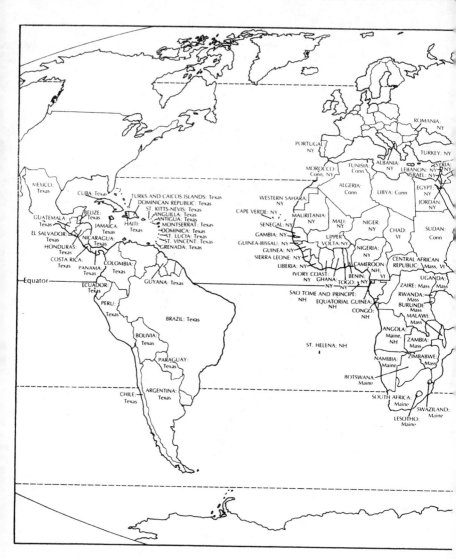

Polar Quartic Equal Area Projection

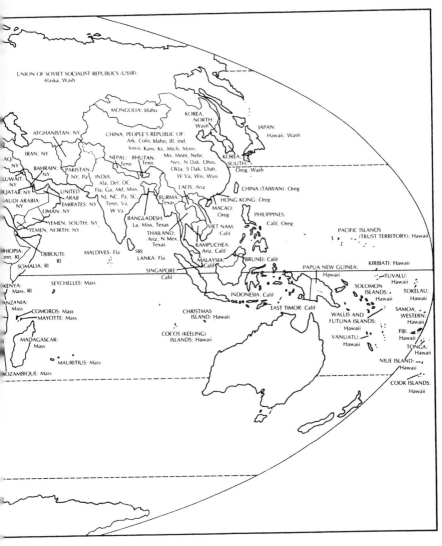

UNION OF SOVIET SOCIALIST REPUBLICS (USSR):
Alaska, Wash

MONGOLIA: Idaho

KOREA,
NORTH:
Wash

JAPAN:
Hawaii, Wash

AFGHANISTAN: NY

CHINA, PEOPLE'S REPUBLIC OF:
Ark, Colo, Idaho, Ill, Ind,
Iowa, Kans, Ky, Mich, Minn,
Mo, Mont, Nebr,
Nev, N Dak, Ohio,
Okla, S Dak, Utah,
W Va, Wis, Wyo

KOREA,
SOUTH:
Oreg, Wash

IRAN: NY

NEPAL: BHUTAN:
Tenn   Tenn

BAHRAIN: PAKISTAN:
NY   NY, Pa INDIA:
Ala, Del, DC,
Fla, Ga, Md, Miss,
NJ, NC, Pa, SC,
Tenn, Va,
W Va

CHINA (TAIWAN): Oreg

AQ
NY

KUWAIT:
NY

QATAR: NY   UNITED
ARAB
SAUDI ARABIA: EMIRATES: NY
NY

OMAN: NY

YEMEN, SOUTH: NY,

YEMEN, NORTH: NY

LAOS: Ariz

BURMA:
Texas

HONG KONG: Oreg

MACAO:
Oreg

PHILIPPINES:
Calif, Oreg

PACIFIC ISLANDS
(TRUST TERRITORY): Hawaii

BANGLADESH:
La, Miss, Texas

THAILAND:
Ariz, N Mex,
Texas

VIET NAM:
Calif

ETHIOPIA:
onn, RI   DJIBOUTI:
RI

SOMALIA: RI

MALDIVES: Fla   SRI
LANKA: Fla

KAMPUCHEA:
Ariz, Calif

BRUNEI: Calif

PAPUA NEW GUINEA:
Hawaii

KIRIBATI: Hawaii

SINGAPORE:
Calif

MALAYSIA:
Calif

SEYCHELLES: Mass

TUVALU:
Hawaii

KENYA:
Mass, RI

SOLOMON
ISLANDS:
Hawaii

TOKELAU:
Hawaii

ANZANIA:
Mass

COMOROS: Mass
MAYOTTE: Mass

CHRISTMAS
ISLAND: Hawaii

INDONESIA: Calif

EAST TIMOR: Calif

WALLIS AND
FUTUNA ISLANDS:
Hawaii

SAMOA,
WESTERN:
Hawaii

VANUATU:
Hawaii

FIJI:
Hawaii

MADAGASCAR:
Mass

COCOS (KEELING)
ISLANDS: Hawaii

TONGA:
Hawaii

NIUE ISLAND:
Hawaii

MAURITIUS: Mass

MOZAMBIQUE: Mass

COOK ISLANDS:
Hawaii

SOURCE: This volume, Appendix B.

CHAPTER 9

Applying the Fruits of Production

Fruits of production

What kind of resources do U.S. Christians have to apply to the world mission task? It is interesting to note when reading the New Testament that the focus of admonitions about resources is on the fruits of production. Jesus consistently addressed the topic of what his followers should do with the resources already in their possession. The New Testament writers continue this theme. Paul urges Christians to work for what they get but many more verses refer to how to be responsible with what one already has. The preoccupation is not with acquiring more but being faithful with what one has.

In a society that spends a great deal of time debating the value of various theories of the best means of production, the Biblical emphasis on fruits of production should be given some thought. Perhaps mission giving suffers because the discussion of the use of the fruits of our production is not accorded the same significance, vitality or emotion that accompanies the ongoing debate about the best means of production.

Applying the fruits of production

Jesus' commands are fairly straightforward to the concerned Christian about distribution of the fruits of production: feed, clothe, share with the brother/neighbor in need. While few would argue that the Christian should pursue these specific acts in some form of charity,[1] what is not clear is what relationship these individual acts of charity have to the incredible need the Christian finds throughout the world.

Evangelism need

Over half the world's population, that is, 2,500,000,000 people live outside the circle of effective gospel witness.[2] Two-thirds of the world's people do not confess Jesus Christ as

Lord and Savior.[3] Over 60,000 people die daily[4] who have not received an adequate presentation of the gospel of Jesus Christ.

What missions activity there is does not focus on the greatest need for the most part. One source " . . . indicated that only 25 percent of the total missionary force were involved in establishing new churches and that the majority of these 25 percent were working in areas where the national church was already established . . . "[5]

Not enough funds are available for mission activity, whether for support of either cross-cultural or indigenous mission work.[6]

Among Third World Christians there was in the past a call for a moratorium on Western mission efforts; there appear to be changes in this trend. In Africa, for example, doors are opening once more. "In a reversal of policy, the new General Secretary of the All Africa Conference of Churches has called for renewed financial support from Western churches. In the past the All Africa Conference of Churches was inclined to downplay the need for outside assistance, in a move to rid itself of the 'stigma' of being a 'missionary' target of Western churches . . . " The secretary general " . . . voiced the hope that the conference would develop into a 'mature partner' of Western churches, but not at the expense of its authentic African nature."[7]

Having had the Great Commission of Matthew 28:18 for 2,000 years, it seems as though the church still has much to do.

Material need

In addition to the great evangelism task, the physical conditions of many of the world's citizens are desperate. Estimates are that 10,000 people daily die from starvation[8] and 40,000 children die each day from poverty conditions.[9]

There is no question in our minds that serious need also exists within the confines of the United States. One need only consider America's inner cities, Appalachia and the needs of elderly citizens on fixed incomes to be convinced of the existence of domestic distress. Internal needs within the U.S. must be addressed by a concerned and caring church. Yet statistics indicate that there are compelling circumstances in the developing world which demand increased attention.

The World Food Council of the United Nations estimated in 1981 that one billion people were hungry.[10] This estimate becomes more difficult to digest when one focuses on the fact that many of those affected by this hunger are children.

Diseases combined with nutritional deficiency result in the statistic that up to one-third of all children born alive in developing countries die before they reach age 5. Many others who survive have their mental development irreversibly impaired by poor nutrition.[11] Millions of people become deaf mutes each year and suffer from endemic goiter for lack of iodine and over 500 children a day become blind for lack of vitamin A.[12]

Such facts as these tend to devalue a human life in the developing world. "One Latin American clergyman reportedly did not register children until they were two years old 'because so many die before that it isn't worth it.' In parts of Ghana the naming of a child is postponed eight days; if it does not survive that long, it is not counted as a birth."[13] A friend of ours returned from Brazil and described a visit to a mother in a *favela* (slum) with a one year old baby who had not yet been named. The woman's child had died a few days before. Touched by the sadness of the fact that the child had lived such a short time, had not even been allowed the personhood of a name, our friend began to cry. The neighborhood women who gathered to see this North American thought she must be extremely tenderhearted to cry for a child she did not even know. Rarely, she was told, does anyone but the mother weep for a dead child because the experience is so common.

And yet, as Christians, it is our faith that Jesus weeps for each one, and that God cared enough to send His Son into the world for each one such as these.

Meeting the needs

Addressing the evangelism needs of the world is clearly within the realm of word mission. Deed mission is alternately referred to as development, pursuit of justice or social transformation.

Secular experts use various categories to estimate the cost of meeting these material needs. For example, in the book, *North-South, A Program for Survival,* (the Report of the Independent Commission on International Development Issues, under the Chairmanship of Willy Brandt) it is estimated that $10–$50 billion a year will address the development needs of the world.[14] The upper end of the range in 1983 dollars would be somewhat over $60 billion. James Grant, Executive Director of UNICEF, stated that by the late 1990's, annually $6 billion could eliminate 20,000 of the 40,000 daily deaths of Third World children.[15]

One source states that:

"Six diseases, measles, poliomyelitis, tuberculosis, diptheria, whooping cough and tetanus are child killers. The World Health Organization estimates that every minute 10 children may die as a result of these diseases. Although vaccines have existed for decades, only 10 percent of the 80 million children born yearly in the developing world are immunized. Cost of immunization is $3.00 per child . . .

"Unsafe water is a factor in 80 percent of all infectious diseases. Over half the population of the Third World lacks an adequate supply of safe water; even larger numbers are without sanitation facilities. Water taps and sewage systems could halve the incidence of diseases like typhoid, dysentery, cholera and schistosomiasis. Seven billion dollars over ten years would provide safe water for all."[16]

Hidden billions

Billions of dollars for water. Billions of dollars for health. Billions of dollars, billions of dollars, the concerned Christian is stopped in his or her tracks. What relevance can Jesus' simple admonitions to feed the hungry have to the overwhelming need that is made more impossible by these statistics?

It is not God's way to ask something of his followers that they cannot, in fact, do. As Paul assures us in 2 Corinthians 9:8.

> *And God is able to provide you with every blessing in abundance, so that you may always have enough of everything and may provide in abundance for every good work.*

Taking this verse to heart, we gathered statistics on Christian giving in the U.S. and came to a conclusion which, given this promise, should not be a surprise: the U.S. church has the resources to help meet these evangelism and social transformation needs. And what is the mechanism for gathering these resources: sacrificial lifestyle? giving up all but the barest necessities? being burdened so that others may be eased?

No.

The U.S. church could increase present local church programs, meet word and deed mission needs and even have money to apply to need within the U.S. through an old-fashioned concept called the tithe.

CHAPTER 10
Kingdom of God Economics

How does the tithe fit?

The concept of giving 10 percent of one's income to the Lord recurs throughout the Old Testament. Giving the first 10 percent to God would assure the Israelites of God's favor. Malachi preached against the people of Israel when they failed to follow this practice.

When Jesus came, however, there was a certain freedom from the law that accompanied him. His followers did not follow ritual cleansing, he healed on the Sabbath and he quoted Hosea to the Pharisees in Matthew 12:7 " 'I desire mercy, and not sacrifice.'" However, this same Jesus also says, "Think not that I have come to abolish the law and the prophets: I have come not to abolish them but to fulfill them." (Matthew 5:17) Perhaps as Jesus is the fulfillment of the law, the freedom we as his followers have is not to be bound by the law but to exceed it; not to be limited, for example, by the tithe, but to give 15 percent, 20 percent or even 30 percent of our income to God's work as the Lord enables us. As Peter writes, "Live as free men, yet without using your freedom as a pretext for evil; but live as servants of God." (1 Peter 2:16)

Certainly the riches entrusted to Christians in the U.S. church are so abundant that some might seriously consider a second or even a third tithe. However, given the present state of the church, we might do well to limit our present discussion to encouraging more Christians to explore giving 10 percent to kingdom work, as a first step.

Kingdom of God economics

Kingdom of God economics is not defined here as being concerned with whether Christians or the church will own any of this world's businesses or control any of the world's governments through our economic power. Kingdom of God economics does mean that we declare our point of reference to be with Jesus' statements. We must be honest about what our joint resources as Christians are. We must consider how these resources are to be used on behalf of a hurting world. It does mean that we need to have a church-wide awareness of the resources that we Christians have in our pockets and bank accounts and stocks and bonds. Deciding to obey Christ, we must begin to define our priorities as salt of the earth.

Christians in the U.S. live in the richest country in the history of the world. Yet Christian giving is at a small percentage. The average per capita giving of full or confirmed members is less than 2 percent. U.S. Christians must be challenged to take the task of the church more seriously.

Then we need to cease being overawed by the economic power of the kingdoms of Capitalism and Communism. God has provided resources to the church perhaps through an economic system but an economic system cannot therefore command our highest loyalties. There are many billions of dollars that we could use in love for others rather than for ourselves. This change in priorities could have a mighty effect on meeting the evangelism and physical needs of this world. For example, if average Christian giving went up to 10 percent per capita, more than an additional $100 billion a year would be available for use in the kingdom of God. Beginning to focus on a kingdom of God economics means that we need to realize that we, the church, Christ's body on earth, presently have at our disposal billions of dollars to use to help further the kingdom of God on earth. These billions of dollars can be used toward the proclamation of the Gospel and assistance of the needy in various ways.

As we speak of these billions of dollars, we must be sensitive to the fact that there are debates now as to whether the riches accumulated in the U.S. are obtained fairly. Have we obtained these goods by unfairly manipulating others who need these resources? The answers to this and other important questions cannot become clear while we maintain our present mind-set. Again, Jesus' wisdom is evident in addressing those resources we already have, the fruits of production rather than the means of production. If our hearts will change over the use of our present possessions, our minds may open to some of these questions and to the structural systematic changes which might be needed to make things fair for all.

In using these resources as part of the kingdom of God, we will have to keep the need for world evangelism as well as justice clearly in mind. It should be God and our loyalty to him which will set our agenda as we interact with the world. Our values are defined in response to God's commandments rather than a secular economic agenda.

Money possessed by the church
in the United States

More than $100,000,000,000 to $300,000,000,000 is available each year to the Christian church in the U.S. for support of world evangelism and helping the starving and malnourished throughout the world, as well as for needs in the U.S. (see Table A). This $100 to $300 billion is over and above the $21.5 billion potentially available at the 1.6 percent giving level in 1983.[1]

In order to provide an overview of the church's giving potential, Table A presents the projected total dollar amounts which were potentially available in 1983 at varying giving levels. Actual contributions through congregations were estimated at about $21.5 billion. Had giving been at the 10 rather than the 1.6 percent level, an additional $100 billion would have been furnished for spreading the Gospel and attaining justice. The totals in column 2 of Table A, are separated into congregational finance and benevolence categories in columns 3 and 4. Benevolences are defined as all expenses outside the congregation; including local and overseas mission and denominational expenses such as retirement funds, camps, headquarters, etc.

Based on the figures in *North-South, a Program for Survival: The Report of the Independent Commission on International Development Issues,* under the Chairmanship of Willy Brandt, it is estimated that $10–$60 billion a year will address the development needs of this world. By merely giving 10 percent, Christians would have the higher figure and still have billions to address internal development issues within the U.S.[2] (*continued on page 70*)

Table A: Total 1983 Dollar Amounts Potentially Available through U.S. Congregations at Varying Levels of Giving in Accordance with Proposed Allocation Schedule.[3]

Average Contributions of Total Adherents at Varying Levels of Giving Expressed as Percentage of Per Capita Income	Total 1983 Dollar Amounts Potentially Available at Varying Levels of Giving	1983 Dollar Amounts Potentially Available for	
		Congregational Finances	Benevolences
Col. 1	*Col. 2*	*Col. 3*	*Col. 4*
30%	$403,005,000,000	$80,601,000,000	$322,404,000,000
20	268,670,000,000	53,734,000,000	214,936,000,000
17.5	235,086,250,000	47,017,250,000	188,069,000,000
15	201,502,500,000	40,300,500,000	161,202,000,000
12.5	167,918,750,000	33,583,750,000	134,335,000,000
10	134,335,000,000	26,867,000,000	107,468,000,000
9	120,901,500,000	26,867,000,000	94,034,500,000
8	107,468,000,000	26,867,000,000	80,601,000,000
7	94,034,500,000	26,867,000,000	67,167,500,000
6	80,601,000,000	26,867,000,000	53,734,000,000
5	67,167,500,000	26,867,000,000	40,300,500,000
4	53,734,000,000	26,867,000,000	26,867,000,000
3	40,300,500,000	26,867,000,000	13,433,500,000
2.5	33,583,750,000	26,867,000,000	6,716,750,000
2	26,867,000,000	21,493,600,000	5,373,400,000
1.6	21,493,600,000	17,194,880,000	4,298,720,000
1	13,433,500,000	10,746,800,000	2,686,700,000

Using Table A

Table A presents an overview of what the U.S. church could be doing if Christian giving went up and it was applied carefully.

Our estimate is that current U.S. per capita giving for Christian congregation adherents is 1.6 percent (see footnote 3). Therefore, the allocations on Table A at the 1.6 percent level actually represent church giving as projected in 1983 dollars. According to these figures, on the average, 80 percent of adherent per capita giving stayed within the congregation, and 20 percent on the average is used for benevolences.

It is assumed that current church giving allows for continuing the church program and even expanding it.

If giving were to increase to 2.5 percent adherent per capita giving, the 80–20 allocation could still be in effect, producing more income for both congregation in-house programs ($26.8 billion as opposed to $17.2 billion) and increased benevolence giving ($6.7 billion as opposed to $4.3 billion). As giving increases beyond 2.5 percent however, the assumption is made that congregation in-house activities have been met and any new money generated should be earmarked for benevolences, with a special emphasis on overseas missions. Based on this assumption, at the 10 percent adherent per capita giving level, 20 percent of the giving is staying within the congregation, and 80 percent is earmarked for benevolences. The 80–20 congregational/benevolences allocation thus becomes 20–80 at the 10 percent giving level.

Initially, as U.S. adherent per capita giving increases, both congregational in-house budget and benevolence budgets increase until the 25 percent giving level is reached. Then, only the benevolences budget increases until the 10 percent giving level. Above the 10 percent level, the 20 percent congregational finances and 80 percent benevolences allocations are maintained as the adherent per capita giving increases past this point.

It is evident that many additional billions of dollars could be available for church use as adherent per capita giving increases.

Current giving

Church congregational per capita giving in 1980 was at about the 1.6 percent level. This 1.6 percent level of giving is obtained by assuming that per capita individual adherent giving through Christian congregations totaled about $17 billion in 1980 with U.S. Christian congregational adherent population totalling somewhat over 113 million. Assuming the 1.6 percent giving level remained constant in 1983, giving through Christian congregations totaled $21.5 billion.

Church officials may point out that not all reported membership is active and that a small percentage of the church membership actually contributes most of the money. On a theoretical level, one wonders if giving would increase if church members were more fully challenged with meeting world needs. On a practical level, some denominations are able to approach 10 percent giving. Denominational memberships range in giving level from around 6 percent at the upper end to around 1 percent at the lower end of the total range (see Table B).

Contrast this church giving with other expenses of the American public. In 1981, Americans including churched Americans, spent 80 times more money on leisure activities than on mission. *U.S. News and World Report* estimated that Americans (half of whom are churched) would spend $244 billion on leisure activities in 1981, with a military budget of $170–180 billion for the same period. Following is a partial listing of 1980 leisure expenditures:

> $8.6 billion on sporting goods
> $7.3 billion on new and used boats, accessories, safety
>   equipment, fuel docking, maintenance and repairs
> $2.0 billion on recreational vehicles
> $2.6 billion on movie tickets
> $25.0 billion on stereos, televisions, and video games
> $4.5 billion on plants[4]

In comparison, missions giving in 1981 was considerably less than $2 billion. (*continued on page 74*)

Table B: Data and Rank Order for 42 Denominations:[5] 1) Per Capita Adherent Contributions and 2) Per Capita Adherent Contributions Used for Benevolences.

Denomination	Year	Per Capita Adherent Contributions Expressed as a Percentage of Per Capita Income			
		Total[6] *Col. 1*	Rank *Col. 2*	Benevolences[7] *Col. 3*	Rank *Col. 4*
Evangelical Church of North America	1980	6.38%	1	1.18%	9
Seventh-day Adventist	1980	6.05	2	4.20	1
Free Methodist Church of North America	1978	6.00	3	1.78	4
Evangelical Mennonite Church	1980	5.80	4	2.35	3
Missionary Church	1980	5.37	5	2.76	2
Presbyterian Church in America	1980	5.03	6	1.35	8
The Evangelical Covenant Church of America	1980	4.85	7	1.13	10
Evangelical Mennonite Brethren Conferences	1980	4.56	8	1.52	5
Mennonite Brethren Churches, General Conference of	1980	4.16	9	1.38	7
The Orthodox Presbyterian Church	1980	4.10	10	.78	12
The Christian & Missionary Alliance	1980	4.07	11	.77	13
Mennonite Church	1980	3.94	12	1.43	6
Assemblies of God	1974	3.33	13	.41	23
North American Baptist Conference	1980	3.32	14	.80	11
Presbyterian Church in the United States	1980	3.01	15	.58	16
Reformed Church in America	1980	2.68	16	.53	17
Church of the Nazarene	1980	2.56	17	.33	28
The United Presbyterian Church in the U.S.A.	1980	2.54	18	.43	22
Evangelical Congregational Church	1981	2.25	19	.50	19
Church of the Lutheran Confession	1980	2.20	20	.48	20
Evangelical Lutheran Synod	1980	2.12	21	.45	21
Church of the Brethren	1980	2.11	22	.59	15

(continued on next page)

Table B: Data and Rank Order for 42 Denominations:[5] 1) Per Capita
(con't.) Adherent Contributions and 2) Per Capita Adherent Contributions Used for Benevolences.

| | | Per Capita Adherent Contributions Expressed as a Percentage of Per Capita Income | | | |
| | | Total[6] | Rank | Benevolences[7] | Rank |
Denomination	Year	Col. 1	Col. 2	Col. 3	Col. 4
The Schwenkfelder Church	1981	2.10	23	.52	18
Cumberland Presbyterian Church	1980	2.10	23	.31	29
Friends United Meeting	1980	2.04	25	.40	26
Moravian Church in America, Northern Province	1980	1.99%	26	.28%	33
Wisconsin Evangelical Lutheran Synod	1980	1.98	27	.41	23
Reformed Church in the United States	1980	1.97	28	.60	14
Christian Church (Disciples of Christ)	1980	1.97	28	.28	33
The Episcopal Church	1980	1.91	30	.30	31
General Baptists, General Association of	1980	1.88	31	.18	40
Lutheran Church-Missouri Synod	1980	1.83	32	.27	35
Moravian Church in America, Southern Province	1980	1.82	33	.41	23
The American Lutheran Church	1980	1.69	34	.29	32
Lutheran Church in America	1980	1.65	35	.31	29
United Church of Christ	1980	1.62	36	.22	38
Church of God (Anderson, Indiana)	1980	1.60	37	.27	35
Southern Baptist Convention	1980	1.57	38	.25	37
The United Methodist Church	1979	1.48	39	.34	27
American Baptist Churches in the U.S.A.	1979	1.39	40	.21	39
The Protestant Conference (Lutheran)	1980	1.32	41	.13	42
The Latvian Evangelical Lutheran Church in America	1980	1.20	42	.16	41

Using Table B

Table B lists the adherent per capita percentage giving for 42 denominations.

The number in the Total Column (Col. 1) is the average percentage of the individual's per capita income given to that church. The number in the Benevolences Column (Col. 3) is the average percentage of the individual's income going for Benevolences. The Benevolences percentage is part of the Total giving percentage.

For example, the average member of the Free Methodist Church of North America gives 6.0 percent per capita to the church (Col. 1). The per capita percentage of the member's giving that goes to Benevolences (Col. 3) is 1.78 percent. Therefore, one can figure that 4.22 percent per capita giving goes for congregational finances (not shown). One can calculate from these figures that 30 percent of the total giving (1.78 ÷ 6.0 = 30) goes for benevolences, ranking the Free Methodist Church third in Total Giving and fourth in amount spent on Benevolences.

By referring to Table C, one can calculate that at 6 percent per capita giving, ideally 67 percent could be going for Benevolences of the Free Methodist Church.

Now if Christians implemented Jesus' commands to love our neighbor in a more sacrificial way, as much as an additional $380 billion, or a 1700 percent increase, in overall giving would be available. That could happen if churched people really decided to live for others and were on the average voluntarily giving at the 30 percent level. This would result in a 7400 percent increase in funds for preaching the gospel worldwide or helping to bring about greater financial equality and justice. A church obeying all that Jesus commands might find amazing resources to apply to the task of evangelism and justice. Even if only one fourth of the church population in the U.S. were to increase giving to 10 percent, there could be an increase of 600 percent in benevolence money for word and deed mission. This amounts to approximately $25 billion in 1983 dollars.

60-20-20

Perhaps current church giving is below 10 percent because many church members are not effectively challenged by the vision of the church. How often have we heard the comment that increased giving to the church will only result in bigger buildings, a newer organ or more staff. Those challenged by meeting world need may wonder if the church is the institution to meet those needs.

This problem may be a matter of pot and kettle calling each other names: church staff may claim members are only challenged by organ funds and something to put a plaque on; church members may complain the contributed money would not make it to missions.

Leaving aside this argument, both staff and members should be challenged by the concept of 60-20-20 as a formula for the congregational budget. If church membership could be challenged to increase giving, careful planning should result in creative application of these resources, yielding more total dollars for the local church, justice concerns within the U.S. and overseas word missions and social transformation.

Currently at the 1.6 percent giving level, an average of 80 percent of the giving stays within the congregation for operating expenses and 20 percent goes for benevolences; i.e., all church related expenses outside the congregation including denominational expenses, camps, retirement funds, overseas and local missions, etc. At the level of 1.6 percent giving, that translates into about $17.2 billion being applied to the local congregation and $4.3 billion going for benevolences (with about $2 billion being expended for overseas mission).

If giving were to increase to 10 percent, self-discipline could be used within the congregation to use only 20 percent within the local church. Then 60 percent could go for overseas missions and an additional 20 percent could go for mission and denominational expenses within the U.S. Even though the local church would be keeping a smaller percentage, the net amount of money would increase. That is, 20 percent of the amount of giving generated at the 10 percent level is $26.9 billion, up from the $17.2 billion generated for the local church at the 1.6 percent giving level. As difficult as it may be for an individual to think about engaging the congregational structure, 60-20-20 is proposed as a congregational budget formula, not as an individual's giving goal.

Figure 1 displays these statistics graphically.

Tables C and D outline how benevolence giving could increase as church giving increases.

Domestic sharing

It is clear from the long tradition of overseas mission how various mission efforts and national churches could apply such increased giving. The yoking concept introduces a format for dialogue on this topic.

It may require some creative thinking on the part of U.S. Christians, however, to apply additional money freed up for domestic sharing. (*continued on page 83*)

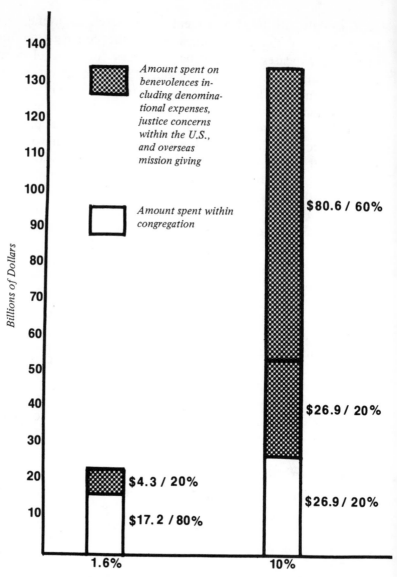

Percentage of Per Capita Giving Level of Church Adherents

Figure 1. Potential of Church Giving at 1.6 and 10 Percent Per Capita Giving Levels in 1983 Dollars.

Table C:[†] Allocation Schedule for Congregational Finances and Domestic and Global Benevolence Expenditures at Varying Levels of Per Capita Giving Based on 20/20/60 Goal Expressed as Percentages of Average Contributions (Col. 1)

Average Contributions of Total Adherents at Varying Levels of Giving Expressed as Percentage of Per Capita Income	Percentage of Average Total Contributions (Col. 1) Available for . . .		
	Congregational Finances	Benevolence Expenditures	
		Domestic*	Global*
Col. 1	*Col. 2*	*Col. 3*	*Col. 4*
30%	20%	20%	60%
20	20	20	60
17.5	20	20	60
15	20	20	60
12.5	20	20	60
10	20	20	60
9	22	20	58
8	25	19	56
7	29	18	53
6	33	17	50
5	40	15	45
4	50	13	37
3	67	13	20
2.5	80	15[8]	5[8]
2	80	15	5
1.6	80	15	5
1	80	15	5

*For a breakdown according to current expenditures and additional money available, see Table D.

[†]For an explanation of Tables C and D see page 80.

Table D:[*] Allocation Schedule for Domestic Benevolence Expenditures

Domestic Benevolences		
	Breakdown of Column 3	
Percentage of Total Contributions Available for Domestic Benevolence Expenditures	Current Priorities Expenditures	Additional Funds Which Would Be Available for Domestic Redistribution
Column 3 from Table C	Column 3a	Column 3b
20%	3.8%	16.2%
20	3.8	16.2
20	3.8	16.2
20	4.2	15.8
19	4.7	14.3
18	5.4	12.6
17	6.3	10.7
15	7.5	7.5
13	9.4	3.6
13	12.5	0.5
15[8]	15.0	0.0
15	15.0	0.0
15	15.0	0.0
15	15.0	0.0

*For an explanation of Tables C and D see page 80.

Table D:[*] Allocation Schedule for Global Benevolence
(*con't.*)   Expenditures

Global Benevolences		
	Breakdown of Column 4	
Percentage of Total Contributions Available for Global Expenditures	Current Priorities Expenditures	Additonal Funds Which Would Be Available
Column 4 from Table C	*Column 4a*	*Column 4b*
60%	1.3%	58.7%
60	1.3	58.7
60	1.3	58.7
58	1.4	56.6
56	1.6	54.4
53	1.8	51.2
50	2.1	47.9
45	2.5	42.5
37	3.2	33.8
20	4.2	15.8
5[8]	5.0	0.0
5	5.0	0.0
5	5.0	0.0
5	5.0	0.0

*For an explanation of Tables C and D see page 80.

Using Tables C and D

At the current level of church giving, money received is allocated as shown at the 1.6 percent level. It is suggested in Table C that the actual amount of money allocated for the category Congregational Finances (Col. 2) should remain constant above 2.5 percent until 10 percent giving is reached. The total amount of money given will be increasing as the average contributor percentage (Col. 1) increases. Therefore, Congregational Finances will be a smaller percentage of the Total as individual giving increases, even though the amount of actual money allocated for Congregational Finances stays the same.

Domestic Benevolence Expenditures allocations (Col. 3) would increase from 15 to 20 percent of the total giving. The dramatic allocation increase would take place in Global Benevolence Expenditures (Col. 4), addressing the world mission task.

At the 10 percent giving level, the formula of 60-20-20 is reached: 60 percent of giving goes for Global Benevolences, 20 percent goes for Domestic Benevolences and 20 percent goes for Congregational Finances. The reader should note that as giving increases from the 1.6 percent level to 2.5 percent, and then above the 10 percent giving level, each category has an increase in the actual amount of money available for expenses.

Table D is a further breakdown of Columns 3 and 4 in Table C. Domestic and Global Benevolences are broken down into current expenditures and additional money which would be available at increased giving levels.

Self-discipline and congregational discipline will be needed to see that the new money available (Columns 3b and 4b of Table D) actually addresses global word and deed mission needs and is available for domestic redistribution. To accomplish this, a few points should be made.

First, additional overhead, that is administrative and fundraising costs at the state and national level, are to be expected when the amount of expenditures increases. However, these overhead expenses should not absorb large parts of this new money if the administrators are going to be faithful to the contributors' wishes. Therefore, it is reasonable to suggest that only 10–20 percent of the increased contributions should go for increased administrative expenses.

Second, Domestic Benevolences Current Priorities Expenditures, although not limited to the following illustrative areas, include such items as camping programs, pastoral retirement, establishing new mission congregations, minority education, seminaries, general denominational administration, some domestic justice issues, etc. The current percentage allotted for these items is noted in Col. 3a. If the congregational members are to be challenged to additional giving, it is important that the increased funds address the needs of the poor in the U.S. Therefore, care must be taken that the increased funds do not expand current priorities (Col. 3a) but actually allow new initiatives for Domestic Redistribution (Col. 3b) to be developed.

Similarly, we assume that the current 5 percent of total contributions designated for Global Benevolence Expenditures would continue to be allocated in roughly the same manner as is currently being done. Such spending includes funds for what may be designated word and deed overseas missions. In the 60-20-20 model represented in these two tables, it is planned that increased global mission giving above the 2.5 percent giving level will go for increased word and deed mission.

Table C presents what might be termed a theoretical or ideal goal with which to evaluate or compare a specific situation. Practical use of Table C requires having some estimate of the giving level of a congregation or denomination. As a hypothetical example, let us assume that a total of 200 men, women and children attend River Falls Church regularly. Let us further assume that one person from each household fills out a slip of paper listing all the income including wages, salaries, interest and/or dividends that was earned by everyone in that household. Now if each piece of paper is turned in anonymously, the total earnings of all those regularly attending River Falls Church can be added up.

Let us say that after each of the papers were turned in anonymously, all earnings were added up and came to $2,000,000. If we know that the church budget is based on contributions of $40,000, then we know that average per capita giving is 2 percent. By looking at Table C at the 2 percent level, we can see in the other columns that we would expect congregational finances to be 80 percent of the total budget or $32,000 and benevolences to be 20 percent or $8,000, with $6,000 going for Domestic Benevolences and $2,000 going for Global.

If however, the River Falls Church decided that they wanted to covenant to give at the 5 percent level during the next year, then, if we assume their total income did not go up and their attendance stays the same, their congregational expenditures would require 40 percent of their budget or $40,000. At this level, $60,000 would now be available for benevolences, $15,000 for Domestic and $45,000 for Global. This $60,000 would be available for expenditures in addition to those required to sustain the congregational building and immediate program. Referring to Table D, one can determine what percent of the $15,000 Domestic or the $45,000 Global Benevolence funds would be available for new outreaches.

In this context, it might be worthwhile to reflect on the idea suggested by some Christian leaders that U.S. Christians should take a more direct role in meeting the needs of poorer U.S. citizens. In fact, John Perkins,[9] Founder of Voice of Calvary Ministries and Mark Hatfield,[10] U.S. Senator, call attention to the fact that there are enough churches in the nation to provide significant financial help to poorer people. This fact received some confused attention in the media in the early '80s but merits closer inspection. There are an average of about 260 active adherents per congregation of historically Christian churches in the U.S. with income levels above poverty level,[11] while there are about 90 persons with income below the poverty line in the U.S. for every Christian congregation in the U.S.[12]

Therefore, there are approximately 3 active church folks above the poverty line for each person in the U.S. below poverty line.[13] Better-off Christians sharing their incomes with people in need, people currently on welfare, could become a natural part of the life of the disciplined Christian congregational life. Certainly such economic sharing with an eye toward equality and fairness would be in the New Testament tradition. Mutual accountability and understanding would grow among those participating in such sharing. God's plan is for people to become involved with each other in order that we change to become more like him. Financial sharing may be a frightening concept but is an important element of demonstrating Christian oneness so that, as Jesus prays in John 17:23, the world will understand that Jesus came from the Father. Thus, love-based sharing between richer Christians and poorer Christians and non-Christians could have a powerful effect. There are enough richer Christians in the U.S. to make a difference in domestic poverty were there the desire and will to do so.

The effects of inflation

For at least the last 20 years, one has heard of the struggle against inflation. We have all experienced a steady rise in prices at the store. Therefore, it comes as a bit of a surprise to realize that in using constant dollars, disposable personal income has increased by about 60 percent from 1960 to 1980. Equally surprising is the fact that, in the same period, per capita full member church contributions in constant dollars have risen only 13 percent.[14]

In the early '60s we already had a relatively high standard of living in the U.S. As our real income increased by 60 percent, we have cited inflation and rising prices as reasons not to increase church giving, while we have in reality spent an increasingly greater portion of the surplus on ourselves. The truth of the matter would appear to be that we have grown in our greed and self-indulgence, the very snare Paul warns against in 1 Timothy 6.

What our giving could accomplish

Current church overseas mission activity involves about $2 billion annually. Consider what a dramatic increase in giving could do.

The U.S. government provided $7.1 billion in 1980 in foreign economic aid, about .28 percent of the gross national product.[15] Private contributions (cash, supplies and equipment) totaling $981 million, were reported in 1981 for American voluntary agencies engaged in overseas relief and development registered with the Advisory Committee on Voluntary Foreign Aid.[16]

It is clear from these figures that even an additional $10 billion given by the church to the church overseas, to help meet the material needs of the poor in Jesus' name and preach the gospel throughout the world could be most significant. An additional $60 billion annually could help even more.

We do not need to be discouraged that Christians are not in full agreement about the best way to do evangelism or to help bring about justice between the rich and the poor. No one involved in such activities claims that they can not use more resources to pursue their approach. Each individual, congregation or denomination can apply the increased giving as deemed best.

Additional money gathered by the church could be used in a variety of complementary ways that reflect the various emphases of the church in the U.S.: word evangelism for those who are not reached with an adequate presentation of the salvation available through Jesus Christ; study of the relationship between preaching the gospel and helping to meet the material needs of the poor; direct food relief where needed; exhortation regarding family planning; increasing education of others in the U.S. regarding adequate water supplies, education, medical assistance and other basic needs overseas; exploring or advocating the need for land reform; or political lobbies on behalf of the oppressed poor throughout the world. Particularly if applied in the Yoking context, the possibility exists that agreement could be reached among the local, national and international partners in the two matched areas.

Impact on U.S. economy

If Christians were to actually share 10 percent of their income, and distribute 60 percent of that giving overseas, there would be a change in the U.S. economy. At the 10 percent level, it may be that the leisure industries would be the first to feel the squeeze. If Christians became more concerned and increased their giving, other parts of the economy would be affected. There are certain points to be made in this regard.

First, if Christians increased their giving out of a conviction that God wanted to pursue justice through his church, we would have to assume that he will provide and maintain a socially ordered system to accomplish this sharing. Peter walked on water until he began debating the practical aspects of it.

On a more practical level, a second point is that such increase in giving would likely take place over a period of time. Great movements have often begun small and gained momentum. As the movement grows, time will be available to provide for the social changes and economic alterations in an orderly fashion.

Third, the society has been able to absorb major changes in the past and found creative responses. The society can rearrange itself for a depression or to wage a war. Certainly, Christians can help society adapt as the church pursues the kingdom of God.

Fourth, again on a practical level, sharing 60 percent of giving at the 10 percent level would mean that U.S. resources would be going overseas at roughly the same level as they were being shared during the Marshall Plan at the end of World War II. At that time, 2.5 percent of the U.S. Gross National Product helped Europe and Japan to reindustrialize and recover from the war, while the U.S. economy continued to grow.[17]

Personal and congregational discipline

It will take personal discipline for the individual Christian to change spending patterns in order to free up 10 percent of his or her income to contribute to the church. In the same way, it will take collective discipline for the congregation to see that overseas and local missions increase. The concerned Christian will want to attend congregational meetings to help set the budget, join the mission committee or the church council, participate in education and stewardship activities to follow the gifts through the church channels. Rather than being seen as an intrusion, it is likely that church staff and the current church leadership will welcome increased interest on the part of the congregational members. If such activity is not welcomed, however, all the more is the increased interest needed.

Focus on money

Money in and of itself is not a solution to material needs and surely not for spiritual needs. Yet insofar as the use of our material resources reflects the desires of our hearts, our use of money has profound spiritual implications.[18] This is most clear in 1 John 3:16–18.

If we are to obey all that Jesus taught us, it is necessary that we use our money and material resources on behalf of others out of love for them. As we bring our intentions and actions into conformity with God's purposes, we can expect an inward change since Jesus tells us that "where your treasure is, there will your heart be also." (Matthew 6:21)

As Christians increase their giving, the world will perceive God acting through his people, who in obedience to Christ use their resources cheerfully and generously for others whom they come to know, understand and love.

PART III

PART III

Previous chapters have focused on the need for personal involvement and have presented large-scale strategies for applying the "hidden billions" to the work of God's kingdom. Certain related concepts remain to be explored.

For example, in Chapter 11, the idea of whether such comprehensive outreach is even possible is considered. The willingness of the church in the U.S. to act on Jesus' commands and the practical implications of such help are discussed.

Chapter 12 reflects on the role of politics in striving to meet the needs of others. What should be the agenda of the church and what is the role of government?

Often, the discussion of helping others on a worldwide basis introduces the debate on the value of certain economic theories. In Chapters 13 and 14, a perspective on the kingdoms of Capitalism, Communism and God is presented. The conclusion is that it is only in the kingdom of God that the concepts of freedom and equality are potentially balanced.

CHAPTER 11

"Stir Up One Another to Love and Good Works"

Doomsayers

In presenting this vision of 10 percent giving and of the impact on world need that a concerned church could have, secular and Christian listeners have had the same response: "It will never happen." The conviction and even anger with which this hopeless assessment of the church is voiced leads one to wonder what pain is behind the statements made.

Various defenses are raised as to why such a negative position is taken: Only a few people in any congregation give most of the money; Membership lists often reflect all levels of commitment, the majority having limited participation; The church has never lived up to its potential. Clearly, many individuals we know may love Christ but have had a very negative experience with his organized church.

Political will

Indeed, that this hopeless attitude exists not only in the church but in richer societies in general is affirmed by some who are knowledgeable on the topic.

James P. Grant notes in his *State of the World's Children 1981–82* Report:

"All of the policies designed to meet such needs — switching the emphasis from universities to primary schools, from hospitals to primary health care, from cities to rural areas, from large estates to small farms — are policies which bring more benefits to the children of the poor and can, at the same time, accelerate a nation's economic growth. It is not, in most cases a question of dismantling hospitals, it is a case of reharnessing hospitals and doctors to the needs of the majority — often through the provision of training, referral and back-up services to primary health care workers.

"But while there can be little doubt that switching priority to the majority of children and mothers renders more efficient the process of using available resources to improve the quality of life, such decisions are ultimately political.

"The political will required to invest in the poor majority is perhaps the scarcest resource of all in the struggle for world development."[1]

The North-South Commission indicates that the problem with world need is not the lack of resources, but the lack of desire to address the problem. Even when it is in the best interest of the rich, the 'haves,' to help those in need, action to change poverty conditions is often not taken.

"History has taught us that wars produce hunger, but we are less aware that mass poverty can lead to war or end in chaos. While hunger rules peace cannot prevail . . .

"Mankind has never before had such ample technical and financial resources for coping with hunger and poverty. The immense task can be tackled once the necessary collective will is mobilized."[2]

It appears that the 15 million children under 5 who die every year do so because people with resources do not particularly want them to live.

What do we want?

We went to a little church that was committed to the "prosperity doctrine." The preacher actually said that if people in the congregation would give God $10, God would return the investment 10 fold with $100. The preacher also said that the last thing to be saved about him was his wallet. Once he began giving to God, however, the Lord gave him all kinds of things because the Lord wants his people to prosper.

Members of the congregation started contributing money and went up to the front with prayer requests: a new boat, a raise at work, a new home. Each request was prayed over.

We sat in our seats, troubled. The preacher seemed to base his arguments on Biblical grounds, yet something didn't ring quite true. We tried to keep an open mind but struggled with whether the pastor could be right in his definition of prosperity and abundance.

Suddenly, a thought broke through. The last thing to be saved about the pastor was not his wallet, but his will. The Christian is supposed to apply these promises of God, quoted in his church for personal gain, with a mind renewed in Christ. As Paul writes in Romans 12:2:

> *Do not be conformed to this world but be transformed by the renewal of your mind, that you may prove what is the will of God, what is good and acceptable and perfect.*

Jesus promises that:

> *If you abide in me, and my words abide in you, ask whatever you will, and it shall be done for you. By this is my Father glorified, that you bear much fruit, and so prove to be my disciples. As the Father has loved me, so have I loved you; abide in my love. If you keep my commandments, you will abide in my love, just as I have kept my Father's commandments and abide in his love.* (John 15:7–10)

And what are Jesus' commandments? That we love God and love our neighbor as ourselves. Paul states that God " . . . desires all men to be saved and come to a knowledge of the truth" (1 Timothy 2:4). In a world where a billion of our neighbors live in need so critical we don't even want to think about it, where 2.5 billion people have never heard an adequate presentation of the gospel, are we sure what we want is what God wants?

Need or desire

An interesting point is made by the noted economist, John Kenneth Galbraith. He states that since World War II, for the first time in the history of the world, a majority of people in a society have their basic needs met. The current economy has produced an abundance of resources beyond these basic needs. Accompanying this new wealth has been an advertising industry whose main task has been to create desires and then transform desires into *needs,* personal comfort absorbing this excess wealth.[3]

This theory might explain why Americans including Christians, are richer than ever before, but find it harder to share even a tenth of their income for the needy of the world.

In "being not conformed to this world," the Christian must step back, get a handle on needs as opposed to wants and settle in his or her mind what the mind of Christ might dictate.

The role of the church

One might not expect a secular society to be committed to alleviating suffering and pursuing justice. Its moral base is varied and not all may agree on the value of changing structures on behalf of those in need. Actually, a government may not necessarily be expected to take a moral stand on behalf of the suffering of the world. Governments are entities which gather their strength from people within certain geographical boundaries. The task of the government is to protect the rights of the people within its boundaries and preserve order. In its simplest form, a government succeeds if it makes people as safe and secure within its boundaries as possible, regardless of its effect on people outside. More specifically, government is most responsive to those sections of its people who have the most power, which is often related to accumulated wealth. These groups are the ones who in fact control the government and influence its course. The powerless may be a minority in a given country. It is not surprising, therefore, that those with wealth use their influence on government to protect their wealth. Government can serve not as a tool for the rights of the poor, but a stabilizing factor for the well-to-do.

On the other hand, one may rightly expect a commitment to those in need from believers in Jesus Christ, that is the church or body of Christ. Members of the body of Christ confess to have gone through or to be in the process of going through, a change of heart. The Christian is to view the world in both its spiritual and physical components in the context of his or her faith. The Christian uses the Bible as a guide for obeying all that Jesus taught us. Our purpose is not to protect what we own but to be faithful disciples of Jesus Christ.

According to Scripture, it is possible for Christians to ignore God's will even as we pursue our own salvation. James is writing to rich followers of Jesus when he admonishes them that they have " . . . lived on the earth in luxury and in pleasure; you have fatted your hearts in a day of slaughter . . . " (James 5:5). And there is that troubling section in Matthew 25: "Lord, when did we see you hungry . . . ?"

As Christians partake of salvation, they ought to be yeast in the dough of society. Yet if Christians opt to take advantage of spiritual blessings with a secular mind, the Christian church will not be distinguishable from society at large. Christianity becomes a gimmick to succeed in the world and not a life-changing force.

The prosperity doctrine at the church we visited is not unique. True, most of the American Christians would not state this philosophy as bluntly, but why is there little more desire in the church than in the world to preach the gospel or meet people's needs? It is a comfortable church which allows the world's children to starve.

The change of heart which changes spending patterns need not go against culture. One need not become a radical, denying the value of the unredeemed society or even the church, and forming isolated communities which maintain the truth in a sterile and pure atmosphere. As salt of the earth we Christians are to be in the world and not of it. Our changed hearts are to lead to changed wills which lead to obedience, particularly in our spending patterns. Such visible obedience can then in fact have a massive impact on society. The overflow effect may result in actually altering the social structures which are in fact unfair. Old and New Testament verses carry forth this theme.

Take for example, God's command to the people of Israel in Deuteronomy 15. First, in verses 1-3, the cancellation of debt every seven years is commanded. Perhaps realizing the fear such a strange economic policy would create, a promise follows in verses 4 and 5: "But there will be no poor among you (for the Lord will bless you in the land which the Lord your God gives you for an inheritance to possess), if only you will obey the voice of the Lord your God, being careful to do all this commandment which I command you this day."

Continuing with admonitions on how to treat the poor in verses 7-10, the point is then made in verse 11. "For the poor will never cease out of the land; therefore I command you, You shall open wide your hand to your brother, to the needy and to the poor, in the Land."

There will be no poor if the Israelites will obey in verse 4, but, perhaps anticipating the lack of collective will, verse 11 notes that there will always be poor and therefore states how to proceed. The presence of the poor is not a comment on the poor's situation but rather is a bellweather of the obedience of God's people.

The fact that God cares about the poor, that God desires that their needs be addressed, is a theme that continues through the Old Testament and into the New. From the proverb that he who is kind to the poor lends to the Lord (Proverbs 19:17) to Isaiah's declaration of the true fast that God wants (58:6-10), there is a clear indication that God expresses a concern for those who do not have resources and requires action from those who are in a position to help.

In the New Testament, starting with the Gospels, direct action is encouraged on behalf of those in need. Jesus' declaration of his ministry focuses on the poor (Luke 4:18-19). When followers of John the Baptist come to ask Jesus if he is the Messiah, Jesus' response includes these signs: the blind receive sight, the lame walk, those who have leprosy are cured, the deaf hear, the dead are raised, and the good news is preached to the poor (Luke 7:22).

Much of Jesus' teachings, and the writings which comprise the New Testament, address the topic of lifestyle for the followers of Jesus. Based chiefly on love for God and for one's neighbor, the focus on material goods is not on protection of goods owned but how they can be used for the good of others. The collective will of the disciples of Jesus should be to use resources available on behalf of those in need.

Do not store up for yourselves treasures on earth, Jesus advises, but store up treasures in heaven (Matthew 6:19-20). "Watch out! Be on your guard against all kinds of greed; a man's life does not consist in the abundance of his possessions . . . Sell your possessions and give to the poor. Provide purses for yourselves that will not wear out . . . " (Luke 12:15, 33 NIV).

The Pauline letters reflect a consistent concern that one's lifestyle be focused on helping others with any resources available. In 2 Corinthians 8:13-15, Paul calls for material equality among believers. In Galatians 6:10 he advises us to do good unto all people, especially to those of the household of faith. Paul notes in Ephesians 2:8-10 that we are saved by grace in order to walk in good works which God prepared for us to do. The love of money is warned against in 1 Timothy 6:9-10. The Christian lifestyle, according to Paul, is to be content with food and raiment; those with resources beyond this are to be rich in good deeds, generous and willing to share (1 Timothy 6:8, 18).

The wisdom of these warnings about preoccupation with material wealth seems very relevant today. Little distinction can be seen between the Christian consumer and the secular consumer: both respond to the temptation to consume for oneself.

Yet the unchanging Word of God continues to point another direction: give and lend and share. To do otherwise is to open oneself to "many griefs" (Luke 16:13, 1 Timothy 6:10 (NIV) John 3:19, James 5:1-6, Revelation 3:14-18).

A new lifestyle

Jesus and New Testament teaching in general indicate that if we have abundance and some have lack, we should give things or money we possess to others out of love for them. Yet as Christians we need to keep in mind that living at some lesser level, consuming less, is not good in and of itself. God created the world to be enjoyed. However his desire is not that some would benefit and others would be hurt. Rather we need to want to use less for ourselves so that others will have a more fair amount of this world's goods. In most cases in the U.S., this will require that we Christians develop the discipline of selflessly giving relatively large amounts to others in need, giving money that could be spent on personal indulgences. We are freed to resist gluttony voluntarily while others can benefit from our excess.

In most areas of life we set goals and guidelines for ourselves. We decide to lose so much weight, improve the yard or home, try to exercise a certain amount or get in so much reading. In our relationship with God, we urge each other to take a certain amount of time for prayer and Bible reading or to gather together a specific number of times for worship, perhaps once or twice a week. Although none of these things are laid out this specifically in the New Testament, we try to discipline ourselves in certain ways while avoiding legalism.

It is in this spirit that we must approach our need to become disciplined givers to others in Jesus' name. We need to discipline ourselves to become generous givers with cheerful hearts so that there may be equality.

As we try to order our stewardship of money, we most likely will be helped if we try to set goals and guidelines for ourselves, much as we do in most areas of life. Compared to the rest of the world we in the U.S. are very rich. Therefore, it would seem that budgeting our income and giving at least 10 percent to assist the needy of this world should be the rock-bottom bare minimum in most cases. How the remaining 90 percent is spent can be left to the individual's discretion.

Is helping practical?

Apart from the Biblical admonition, the practical person may resist helping those in desperate need overseas because saving the starving will only mean more people on a planet whose resources are already strained. These people may say that in fact (though many are children) starving is nature's way of evening out the resources. Overpopulation among humans, like rats, results in some dying until the balance is restored.

Christians can resist this thinking on several grounds. First, Christians do not serve a goddess called "nature" who in an unfeeling way sets checks and balances in motion. On the contrary, the Father God is one who loves the world enough to send his own Son on its behalf. That Son, Jesus Christ, declares that the Father cares for the birds of the air: "Are you not of more value than they?" (Matthew 6:26). In such verses as Matthew 25:31–46 and 1 John 3:16–18, it is these very people, the starving ones, that rich Christians are admonished to love as neighbor and to help.

C.S. Lewis was able to translate this concept into a concise thought.

> "The load, or weight, or burden of my neighbor's glory should be laid daily on my back, a load so heavy that only humility can carry it, and the backs of the proud will be broken. It is a serious thing to live in a society of possible gods and goddesses, to remember that the dullest and most uninteresting person you talk to may one day be a creature which, if you saw it now, you would be strongly tempted to worship, or else, a horror and corruption such as you now meet, if at all, in a nightmare. All day long we are, in some degree, helping each other to one or the other of these destinations. It is in light of these overwhelming possibilities, it is with the awe and the circumspection proper to them, that we should conduct all our dealings with one another, all friendships, all loves, all play, all politics. There are no *ordinary* people . . ."[4]

Yet 17 million of these potential gods or goddesses are in the world less than five years, some passing through without the dignity of a given name.

We Christians do not have to extend help to others only as a matter of faith however. For example, assisting the dying poor will not necessarily create overpopulation. Quoting at some length from his 1982–83 report *State of the World's Children,* it seems James P. Grant has one of the most concise answers to this argument:

"At this point, an obvious question arises from the apparent conflict between this potential 'survival revolution' and the need of the majority of developing countries to slow down their rates of population growth. But it is a conflict which is dissolved by time. For when people become more confident that their existing children will survive, they tend to have fewer births. That is the principal reason why no nation has ever seen a significant and sustained fall in its birth rate without first seeing a fall in its child death rate.

"Historically, when overall death rates make that first steep fall from aroung 40 per 1,000 as a result of eliminating epidemics, the decline in birth rates follows a long way behind. The result is rapid population growth. Fortunately, history has also shown, in the era since World War II, that when overall death rates have fallen to around 15 per 1,000 people — which, significantly, is about the average for the low-income developing countries today — then each further fall of one point in the death rate has usually been accompanied by an even larger fall in the birth rate. Thailand's 7 point fall in death rate (from 15 to 8 per 1,000) between 1960 and 1980, for example, was accompanied by a 14 point fall in the birth rate. In the same period, Costa Rica's 5 point fall in death rate (from 10 to 5 per 1,000) was accompanied by an 18 point fall in the birth rate. Similarly, an 8 point fall in the death rate of the Philippines was accompanied by a 12 point fall in birth rates.

"Paradoxically, therefore, a 'survival revolution' which halved the infant and child mortality rate of the developing world and prevented the deaths of six or seven million infants each year by the end of the century, would also be likely to prevent between 12 and 20 million births each year.

"The availability of family planning can shorten the time-lag between falling death rates and falling birth rates."[5]

There are other logical arguments which support the concept that help is not only necessary but in our own self-interest. At a major university conference on world food trade systems, speaker after speaker noted that the lack of food is a major factor in producing violent revolution around the world.[6] Think of countries which have been involved in intense internal conflict in recent years and how major a part people's basic needs played in the struggle. People desperately in need contribute to an unstable world reality which affects all the earth's inhabitants.

The issues regarding how best to help these dying children and their families are extremely complex. The solution in the past of just sending resources without concern for the internal effect on the receiving countries has been criticized. Such aid can actually support unjust governments and help people in need only barely enough to keep them alive. Some people assert that sharing resources is not the need as much as changing the system to make it easier for everyone to have access to the resources.

An official of the World Bank comments on the concerns of people in the Third World that the whole topic of basic needs " . . . may be used by the developed countries to divert attention from the North-South dialogue on the New International Economic Order." This official describes the concern as being that the developed countries will begin by addressing the topic of basic needs but that the donors will then try to

" . . . tell the developing countries to reform their own national priorities before they question the inequities of the international system."[7]

Shifting resources may be only a first step toward meeting world need. It does allow those actually sharing the resources to become personally involved in the problem. As we become involved, we will no doubt become aware of what complexities are involved and apply our best energies to exploring solutions. In the short-term it may also provide immediate hope to those in desperate need.

But as we become personally involved, it is possible that other issues will come into focus. The issue of ownership of the resources is raised by some economists as a major issue, including those at the Institute for Food and Development Policy. In *Food First: Beyond the Myth of Scarcity,* members of the Institute consider the issues involved in world need along these lines: "The root cause of hunger has to do with the relationships of people to each other and to the control over basic resources. As long as people think the fundamental causes are elsewhere, this root cause will go neglected and people will in fact become hungrier."[8]

The need to grow beyond just sharing resources to understanding root causes must happen. However a good first step might be obedience to Jesus in the seemingly simple task of sharing our goods. "And be sure to put into practice what you hear. The more you do this, the more you will understand what I tell you," Jesus promised (Mark 4:24 LB).

What more exciting time to be alive than now, when the need has never been clearer and the resources greater. What an exciting prospect to see what even 10 percent can do!

CHAPTER 12
Where Do Politics Fit?

Charity Ghetto/Political Penthouse

Thus far in the discussion, we have focused on what Christians can do through direct action, whether through personal involvement or sharing 10 percent or more of the individual's income. Little has been said about pursuing justice through politics.

Our view is that as Christians pursue justice through individual discipleship, there will be a natural overflow into the political arena. One does not organize the church as a means to a political end. However, if Christians are living their lives for others in a disciplined way, it is likely that these convictions will show up at the voting booth in this democracy.

Too often, as soon as a Christian becomes concerned, however, s/he feels that individual acts of charity lead no place. Direct discipleship is relegated to "the charity ghetto." Unaware of the figures of what Christians can accomplish by combining even 10 percent of their income, the concerned Christian turns to politics. Because politics are so far removed from the daily lives of most people, the lobbying, letter-writing and other activities take place in a rarified atmosphere which might be termed "the political penthouse."

The church's agenda

Focusing on politics can be an academic and divisive activity as well. In our experience, we have been able to gather Christians from various backgrounds in a room to discuss how to feed hungry people or how to bring black and white Christians together. As long as we stay focused on the task at hand, and on a Biblical basis, action results in the need being met. The very act of meeting the need educates the doer and perhaps breaks down some stereotypes which formerly closed that Christian's mind on some issue.

However, as soon as a particular candidate or particular party's platform enters the discussion, the room can divide into camps, the agenda becomes an academic debate, no action results and the needs remain unmet.

We do not want to imply that Christians should stay out of politics. However, if the church worried first about establishing its own agenda, it could function better in "leavening the whole loaf."

What is the role of government?

It is clear that Christians in the U.S. cannot ask government to take the good news of Jesus Christ to the unreached people of the world. If we want to see that task accomplished, we who are the body of Christ must do it directly.

The issue becomes less clear when we talk of assisting the poor throughout the world. Government has become large and is involved in many areas of life. It begins to seem to have a life of its own, apart from the people who are the source of government and government programs. Therefore, we fail to realize that no matter how efficient and powerful government is, it will not tend to accomplish a great deal more good than the people of this country want.

For example, if the people of this country do not want to be taxed another $30 billion dollars to assist the more than 500 million people of this world who are in physical need, then most likely, elected representatives will not vote to tax us that additional amount.

On the other hand, if Christians privately raised and used from $10 to $60 billion annually on behalf of the poor throughout the world, we would constitute such an aware, dedicated group within the country that government would by definition be much more responsive to the needs of poor and oppressed throughout the world. As we begin to share our personal income, there would be an outflow into the political arena as concerned Christians used their vote to express their concern for justice.

As a practical consideration, it does not seem likely that we Christians will vote to tax ourselves to assist the poor worldwide in the name of the U.S. government if we will not give our money generously on behalf of the poor in Jesus' name. After all, if out of love we give a cup of cold water to someone — then if given the choice of giving it in Jesus' name or not — it would seem better to give the cup of cold water in Jesus' name. In this way, it may be more likely that the person will drink that water which "will become in him a spring of water welling up to eternal life." (John 4:14)

This is not to deny the role of politics and governments. If we Christians decide to give generously and sacrificially to help the hungry, the sick, the naked and the imprisoned throughout the world, we will find countless ways in which we will want to use our country's government to assist in this effort. Yet we need to put the horse in front of the cart. There may well be an emptiness and hypocrisy in political activity and requests for government action that do not flow directly from our own voluntary outpouring of ourselves in Jesus' love for others. Can we honestly ask a government, which represents both Christians and non-Christians, to take actions that we Christians refuse to take voluntarily in response to Christ's love within us?

Often Christians who become concerned about world need or injustice immediately turn to government to solve the problem. This response is natural since government for a long time has been the visible, organized representative of the people. The church is divided, split up, definitely not cohesive. The difficulty within the church might not even be in raising funds as much as in trying to come to agreement as to how to spend them. Christians may feel a common commitment to work on the Great Commission, but there does not appear to be a firm commitment to do it in an organized and coordinated fashion. As just one example, in one survey of mission organizations, no fewer than 645 Protestant mission agencies are active in 183 countries.[1] Though the U.S. government may be big and cumbersome, it at least has a central office.

Calling the church to accountability

The lack of agreement in the church may make it difficult for the concerned Christian to pursue justice and equality within the congregation. Even in John Wesley's time, it appeared to be difficult for the church to stay loyal to a Biblical agenda:

> "It nearly concerns us to understand how the case stands with us at present. I fear, wherever riches have increased, (exceeding few are the exceptions) the essence of religion, the mind that was in Christ, has decreased in the same proportion. Therefore do I not see how it is possible, in the nature of things, for any revival of true religion to continue long. For religion must necessarily produce both industry and frugality; and these cannot but produce riches. But as riches increase, so will pride, anger, and love of the world in all its branches."[2]

It is this "pride, anger and love of the world in all its branches" which make it difficult for the concerned Christian to turn his or her individual congregation around in a voluntary way. Suspicion and hurt can be the fruit of confronting people face-to-face about their financial obligations as Christians. The authors knew a committed Christian who organized far-reaching relief projects through a secular organization. When asked why he did not combine his social concern with the good news of Jesus Christ by working through his church, he looked surprised at the questioners' ignorance. "It would be impossible to move them an inch," he responded.

Therefore, secular government serves as an attractive alternative to doing the long-term, sometimes painful discipleship required in the church. The theory is that a concerned individual can issue a rallying cry and mount a movement which can eventually enforce justice through taxation or legislation on those who will not voluntarily comply. Yet sometimes those who won't comply on a voluntary basis are the people who share the pew with us on Sunday mornings and join us at the Lord's table for communion.

Unable to work things out believer to believer we enlist Washington, D.C. as a mediator, but lose the ability to give credit to Jesus Christ in the process. Moving politically as a *primary* source of strategy is to concede that the kingdom of God has no basis or foundation within the body of Christ but must be founded through secular government. It is poor political science to ask government to force Christians to do what we won't do voluntarily out of our Scriptural conviction.

An alternative strategy is to begin at the voluntary base and let the resulting good overflow into the secular system. John Wesley's concern caused him to challenge the church to be the church:

> "Is there no way to prevent this? This continual declension of pure religion? We ought not to forbid people to be diligent and frugal: we must exhort all Christians to gain all they can, and to save all they can; that is, in effect, to grow rich! What way then (I ask again), can we take, that our money may not sink us to the nethermost hell? There is one way, and there is no other under heaven. If those who 'gain all they can,' and 'save all they can,' will likewise 'give all they can;' then, the more they gain, the more they will grow in grace, and the more treasure they will lay up in heaven."[3]

Concerned Christians coming to the conclusion that the church should be involved in meeting the need for justice in the world, need not conclude that politics is the first course of action. The simple sayings of Jesus, to love one's neighbor and sell what one has, giving it to the poor, have not proved unworkable — perhaps they have not yet been tried.

CHAPTER 13

The Kingdoms of Capitalism, Communism and God

Three kingdoms

Go therefore and make disciples of all nations, baptizing them in the name of the Father and of the Son and of the Holy Spirit, teaching them to observe all that I have commanded you . . . (Matthew 28:19-20)

With these words, Jesus commissioned his followers to pro-claim the Good News to the world. From that point in Galilee, a movement was spread that would change history. Believers in Jesus would come to influence every nation on earth. The question can be fairly put, however, to what end?

Jesus' injunction to teach "them to obey everything I have commanded you" does not seem to have ensured consistent compliance. Particularly, in the area of economics, the gospel of Jesus has produced confusing fruit. Perceptions about the church in contemporary times provide a chaotic picture.

For example, the United States of America is viewed by some as a Christian nation which combined missionary fervor with Manifest Destiny to exploit many realms of the world. The church in some Third World countries is perceived as an oppressive force by those who feel it supports repressive regimes in their own country. In those same countries, religious figures are seen by other people as troublemakers inciting people to riot with promises of "liberation theology." In the Soviet Union, before the revolution, Christianity was called the opiate of the people, promising a better future to make a horrible present tolerable. Now, religious people are seen as fanatic individualists who are dangerous to the collective economic good.

Why is it so difficult to get a picture of what the church really is offering in terms of economic reality? Does the Bible have nothing to say about the material realm? Is the Good News of Jesus addressed only to the spiritual realm, with economics focused on the physical realm?

The problem may lie at least partly in the fact that Christians have stopped defining themselves in terms of obeying all that Jesus commanded, including his assertions about material reality. Instead, Christians have defined themselves in terms of their secular culture. Religion is then added on to this culture as a refining force. Jesus' commands are no longer the point of reference for most believers but are seen as an influence which must be built into the practical reality of daily life. Yet Jesus Christ did not come to offer a flavoring agent for the secular world. He came to declare the existence of the kingdom of God. Jesus Christ was looking for citizens of this new kingdom who would establish an order on his teachings, " . . . make disciples . . . teaching them to obey everything I have commanded you."

Jesus Christ came to declare the kingdom of God and commands loyalty to the system over which he is Lord. He declares that, "No servant can serve two masters. Either he will hate the one and love the other, or he will be devoted to the one and despise the other. You cannot serve both God and Money" (Luke 16:13 NIV). Jesus asks that his followers declare themselves — they must see God or money as the absolute reference point. Jesus elevates money in this passage to the level of a master, capable of commanding loyalty as does God. In light of this statement, it is not out of line to assert that each person must decide whether he or she is loyal first to the secular material realm or to God. Each person must use as his or her primary frame of reference a secular-economic-political kingdom or the kingdom of God. The two current prevalent economic kingdoms are Capitalism and Communism.

The choice is rarely posed in a clear fashion to the followers of Jesus in the United States of America. People are encouraged to embrace democratic liberalism or socialism on the left. Or people are encouraged to embrace a conservative platform on the right. In neither case is the topic of the significant financial potential of the body of Christ's income and accumulated wealth given serious consideration.

From Luke 16:13, we see that Jesus pits money against God. We should not assume that Jesus was against money itself, however. The disciples held a money purse in common and Judas Iscariot was the treasurer (John 12:6). Jesus paid the tax with the coin from the fish (Matthew 17:27) and holding up a coin, urged people to give unto Caesar what is Caesar's (Matthew 22:21). It is not logical to assume from Luke 16:13 that one must choose between cash or prayer to pay for one's dinner. Rather, Jesus is addressing the topic of lordship: which system will we use to define our behavior? Will we have Jesus serve money or will money serve Jesus?

The confusion about our Christian witness in the world may result because many people are citizens of either the kingdom of Capitalism or Communism, using money as the main reference point. These people then profess Christianity as a good influence on their lives. There was not confusion on Jesus' part as to what the reference point should be. God is to be the Lord of his servants and the use of money is to be dictated by kingdom of God principles.

Both communism and capitalism are powerful forces in this latter part of the twentieth century. These two economic systems take material reality to be the main reality. The debate centers on ownership of the means of production. In the most general sense of the terms, capitalism argues for private ownership and communism argues for public ownership.

Both systems assume humanity, left to itself, will produce an economic environment that maximizes the common good. In capitalism it is asserted that each person seeking his or her own best interests will produce the most products and jobs for the general good. In communism, it is assumed that the worker (proletariat) will grow into responsibly administering the general resources available for the common good. The state owns the means of production in the socialist stage while eventually the people control them under communism.

While both systems use the material, physical world as reality, capitalism and communism emphasize two separate parts of the human dream. Generally speaking, the kingdom of Communism is portrayed as emphasizing equality; the kingdom of Capitalism is offered as emphasizing freedom. It is the kingdom of God which emphasizes a combination of equality and freedom.

In dealing with the above statement and the following comments, one could approach this material from the perspective of the historian, economist, political scientist, philosopher and/or theologian. The present focus is on using very broad categories that seem to be present in the popular understanding of communism and capitalism.[1] This popular understanding of the two basic rival economic-political systems is one of the more significant realities operating today. As we attempt to understand the kingdom of God and Jesus' call to obedient discipleship, we must consider the implications of these other economic realities. These issues are particularly important as we consider the Christian's mandate to preach the Gospel worldwide and address the desperate survival struggle many people face.

The kingdom of Communism

There apparently is no perfect unity and singleness of mind and strategy for worldwide communism with undisputed Soviet leadership. The U.S.S.R. increases its use of grain-fed beef, consumer goods and military power as its wealth increases much in the same fashion as do other developed nations, even while other communist lands have fewer food supplies. Also, there is not financial equality among some of these countries. Consider, for example, the Gross National Product (GNP) levels for various communist countries. While the GNP per capita for the U.S.S.R. is $3700, that of the People's Republic of China is $460, Cuba is $810 and Vietnam is $170.[2] The equality preached in theory is not manifest among nations using the philosophy.

Communist leaders struggle for autonomy from each other or dominion over each other based on centuries-old geographic and nation-state loyalties and rivalries. Although it may not be evident to the average U.S. observer, there is a variety in communism as it is evidenced in Yugoslavia, Hungary, China and Cuba, for example. There are also theoretical differences evident between European Communists and Latin American Marxists.

Communism's concern for equality is perhaps more clearly observed in the context of the North-South disparity than in the East-West belligerence. The North-South struggle focuses on the great inequality between Europe and North America on the one hand and Asia, Africa and Latin America on the other hand. Latin American Liberation Theology, which has been influenced at points by the Marxist dialogue, is sensitive to the gross inequalities operating both within countries and between countries in such areas as trade laws, access to financial markets and commodity agreements. Viewing Latin Americans as romantics, European Marxists may consider themselves to be dealing with more sophisticated matters such as worker alienation stemming from the conflict between skilled and unskilled workers due to the advance of high technology.

In addition, one notes that hybrids of capitalism and communism exist in socialist states. Nevertheless as one observes the continuing worldwide unrest and demand for fairness in material goods distribution, the appeal of the abstract communist claim for equality is evident. A main attractive thrust of communism is the declaration that the downtrodden of the world should be championed. Equality is stressed by communists over freedom at the present time. The leadership is prepared to use the power of the state to enforce equality. The government plans eventually to reach economic equality, accompanied by increased freedom, as the proletariat grows in understanding.

Apart from all the limitations as it is actually implemented, the kingdom of Communism appeals to and stresses that part of the human dream which calls for equality and fairness, even if communism is willing to use force to implement its portion of the human ideal, at the sacrifice of individual freedom and initiative.

The kingdom of Capitalism

On the other hand, the kingdom of Capitalism appeals to that part of the human ideal summarized by the term "freedom."

There is an emphasis on freedom, individual initiative and creativity, and the incentive to excel among capitalists. In the everyday world this translates into the freedom to make as much profit as one can, the assumption being that each seeking his or her best interest will benefit the whole.

In reality, of course, the dream of freedom is not perfectly carried out. The deck gets stacked in any given generation. Those with resources have the freedom to pass on their wealth to their children through inheritances. Those people who do not benefit from inheritances begin with a disadvantage. Not everyone benefits from the free society as the elderly, the inner-city poor and the concentrations of need in Appalachia would attest. The system may not seem to work well. As Dom Helder Camara, Archbishop of Olinda-Recife, Brazil notes "When will we fully understand that 'freedom' is a word without meaning to someone who does not have a house fit to live in, or food fit to eat, or clothes fit to wear, or a minimum of education and decent work?"[3]

In addition, income taxes and partial distribution of wealth through welfare programs and governmental regulations place some limits on pure unrestrained freedom. And preservation of good investment climates, which allows one group to pursue freedom of investment, seems to have led at times to the support of military dictatorships which suppress other people's freedom. A subtle shift takes place from emphasis on freedom to the survival of the fittest. Today the United States faces criticism for supporting governments which serve U.S. business interests rather than emphasizing freedom for all people involved. In addition, strong forces within capitalism (e.g., the drive for the individual to succeed at all costs) compete strongly with the Christian ethic (e.g., love one's neighbor as oneself). This fact can make it very costly to exercise the religious freedom which exists on a theoretical level in capitalism. Loving one's neighbor can actually conflict with succeeding in capitalism.

Yet on the whole, glimpses and portions of the ideal remain untarnished. Many live with the hope and others demonstrate, that in a capitalistic society, regardless of obstacles or lack of privilege at birth, one can rise to the top and give full expression to one's potential. In addition, the democracy of the United States, associated with its capitalistic economy, offers citizens a great freedom not seen in many other parts of the world. Having traveled in Eastern Europe and Latin America, we can testify to the real freedom to speak one's mind and worship God which is available to the U.S. citizen.

Comparisons, contrasts and interaction between the kingdoms of Capitalism and Communism

The kingdom of Capitalism says that, ideally, if each person is engaged in freely pursuing his or her own interests, and is rewarded by other freely moving persons, society as a whole will be most productive and that everyone will be as well off as possible. Thus even most of the people at the botton of the heap in a capitalist society will theoretically have as much or more than people in a centrally planned or communist economy. A communist economy has the heavy hand of the bureaucratic police-controlled state which quenches individual freedom and individual initiative and thus the creative human spirit. According to this view, individual ownership provides a broad base of financial power and thus a broad base of control in society. This diversity of control preserves freedom, particularly religious freedom, which is suppressed in the kingdom of Communism.

However, the kingdom of Communism claims to focus on the reality of the poor and financially oppressed. State enforced equality may in fact reduce the freedom of some who are oppressing others. In theory, however, it allows for greater freedom for those who are oppressed, for those who may not succeed in a capitalistic society. By pushing for economic equality for the poor and those who do not wield power, eventually freedom for all will be maximized, according to this approach.

We are here discussing the broad scale emphases popularly identified with communism and capitalism as they now exist. Capitalism and communism argue that in the long run they each both provide a higher and thus fairer material standard of living for all *and* more freedom than the other. Buckminster Fuller comments on communism's longer term advocacy of freedom:

> "I have only *one* objection to the concept of comprehensive socialism: So far it has made no provision for effective development of the individual initiative of humans. Too long has such freedom of initiative been usurped either by the Communist party, representing only 1 percent of the U.S.S.R. population, or by the Western world's private enterprise's utterly selfish exploitation for money-making rather than for common sense-making. I have discussed this point with the Russians. They admit that a *party* dictatorship is not 'democracy' and, at the same time, also admit that it is for *true* democracy to which the Russians, the Chinese, and most people of the world aspire."[4]

It appears that there is a serious dilemma which faces a person: one must choose individual freedom at the expense of those less able to compete; or one must choose on behalf of the common good and sacrifice various freedoms in the pursuit of equality. Both economic realities would counter criticisms leveled at the possible bad side-effects of their system with the hope of problems working out over time. The capitalist, unless ruthlessly committed to survival of the fittest, assumes that the less fortunate are provided for through the successful capitalist's generosity. The communist believes the proletariat is on its way to perfection. The enforced redistribution of goods will be fair if uncomfortable in the short run, and a new age will dawn in the long run when the state's functions are carried out by the newly arrived proletariat.

It is into this false dilemma — equality or freedom — that the kingdom of God must be introduced. To expose the falseness of this proposed choice is to begin to grasp the very good news of Jesus Christ and his commands. For in the kingdom of God, it is not assumed that human beings, left to themselves, will create any type of happy system. In fact, God found it necessary to intervene in the history of the world, reconcile it to himself and declare a whole new order. It is because man was sinful (Romans 3:23) and loved evil that Jesus was sent as the light of the world to reconcile it to God (John 3:16–21). Within the kingdom, a change of heart is required of each person. And this change would produce an order in which both equality and freedom are maximized.

From a Christian kingdom of God viewpoint, one reflects on the kingdoms of Capitalism and Communism with sadness and concern. It is sad that the world becomes divided with each side grasping one part of the truth. As the principalities and powers of the world embody these two parts of truth with a form of life, the kingdoms of Capitalism and Communism with their ideologies and various expressions become idols worshipped by the world. Neither one is formally offered as a religion and yet their adherents begin to define them as a worldview. Both view materialism as the basic reality of life and both depend on the innate goodness of corporate humanity to keep the system from going astray. Unfortunately the church, for the most part, seems to be confused and caught up in this distortion of the truth. The church in the 20th century does not realize it has a third alternative to offer and merely tries to influence one system or the other.

Both freedom and equality are two lovely ideals that are part of God's kingdom. Yet it seems that as a historical fact, they can be wrenched out of context and worshipped as ideals apart from God who made provision for people to relate to each other in freedom *and* equality. Perhaps we should attempt to look at the kingdom of God with a fresh perspective.

CHAPTER 14
Equality and Freedom

Kingdom of God

It is in Christ and the kingdom of God he proclaimed that we can see equality and freedom in proper relationship to each other.

Jesus declares in John 8:31b–32, "If you continue in my word, you are truly my disciples, and you will know the truth, and the truth will make you free."

The apostle Paul notes that "the law of the Spirit of life in Christ Jesus has set me free from the law of sin and death" (Romans 8:2). This idea is underscored in Galatians 5:2 as Paul declares that "For freedom Christ has set us free."

Yet this freedom exists in the context of the lordship of Christ. Freedom exists for a purpose. Are we free from all rules and guidance, to follow our own desires and lusts? That is not the perspective that Christ gives. Remember that in Matthew 28 Jesus declares that his disciples should obey all that he taught. We are free from sin and death, now free to serve our Lord and King.

It is in this new mind-set that we are free to love and serve not only God but other people. We are in fact even free to lay down our lives for our brothers and sisters (1 John 3:16–17).

Jesus notes in Luke 12:22–32 that we are free from concern about our physical cares — God in fact is going to give us the kingdom. The conclusion of the announcement is that we are therefore free to sell what we have, give it to the poor and follow Jesus (v. 33).

This freedom from concern is noted by Paul about the Macedonian church in 2 Corinthians 8:1–5. Out of their poverty, God has given the grace to the Macedonians to share fully with the believers in Jerusalem. And Paul goes on to urge that the Corinthians complete their act of grace in generous giving (v. 6) not to burden the Corinthans while helping others but that there may be equality (vv. 13–15). Paul understands that freedom in Christ allows us to forgo this world's cares and therefore seek equality of resources within the church and the well-being of those outside (Galatians 6:10).

Let us think of the greatest freedom any government has provided for or legislated. In fact we say that God is the ultimate source of that freedom (Romans 13:1). The United States Declaration of Independence also asserts this concept:

> "We hold these truths to be self-evident, that all men are created equal, that they are *endowed by their creator with certain unalienable rights,* that among these are Life, Liberty and the pursuit of Happiness . . . "

Similarly let us think of the greatest equality we have seen any state call for or implement. Again God has called for that degree of equality and more. Doesn't Paul actually call for equality in 2 Corinthians 8:13–15? When the Holy Spirit was poured out at Pentecost, one manifestation was the sharing of material goods so that any with needs were provided for and poverty was eliminated (Acts 4:32–35). Certainly God intends for both freedom and equality to be maximized in the kingdom of God. Certainly financial equality is not inconsistent with the character of God as evidenced in his grace manifest in Christ Jesus. Spiritual reconciliation and salvation are far more valuable than earthly possessions; this salvation is offered equally to any who would believe (John 3:16; 1 Timothy 2:4). If God is willing to share his precious Son with all on an equal basis, we should not balk at extending our sense of his concern to the physical realm.

In response to those who will quickly quote a scriptural base for an easy acceptance of the poor's continued existence (Matthew 26:11), one may refer to the Old Testament reference for Jesus' quote (Deuteronomy 15:4–11). As has been noted, in this context, Jesus' comment indicates that the presence of poverty is not a necessity as much as a bellweather of whether God's people are obedient to his commandments. Jesus introduces a new factor which is not addressed by either capitalism or communism. To be able to emphasize both equality and freedom, each person must become a new creature in Jesus Christ.

It is through the renewing of each person's mind that freedom becomes not a license for personal excess but a tool through which to love others. Equality is not an idea to be enforced but a goal to be delighted in: God in Christ calls us to lay down our lives for others freely, out of love. In Christ, we are called to live for the other person in a direct active fashion and are given the freedom and ability to do that to the fullest. In 1 Peter 2:16 we are admonished to "Live as free men, yet without using your freedom as a pretext for evil; but live as servants of God." We are not free just to be able to indulge in gluttony and greed. Jesus warns us in Luke 12:15, "Watch out! Be on your guard against all kinds of greed; a man's life does not consist in the abundance of his possessions" (NIV). Rather, we are freed to become citizens of the kingdom of God where the two greatest commandments are to love the Lord our God with all our heart, soul and mind and to love our neighbor as ourselves (Matthew 22:35–40).

So, in the kingdom of God, we find that we can choose to live for others rather than for ourselves; we have freedom and can work for equality out of concern for other people.

In the kingdom of Capitalism citizens grasp for their own freedom with a secondary concern for the well-being of others in the financial area of life. And in the kingdom of Communism, citizens struggle for equality while sacrificing individual freedom for the present, in the hope that freedom will be maximized for all in the future. Only in the kingdom of God, as we submit our will to God's will, do we have the freedom to voluntarily pursue fairness and equality for all.

The church and the kingdoms of
God, Capitalism and Communism

The church as the people of God and literally Christ's body on earth is the agent of the kingdom of God. The church is to be in the world but not of it. As part of being in the world, the church does interact with the kingdoms of Capitalism and Communism. However, the tragedy is that without a clear realization of her own identity, different parts of the church bounce back and forth between capitalism and communism with a maximum of confusion both within and without herself.

One part of the church seeks at all costs to maintain the freedom held out by the kingdom of Capitalism while another part of the church seeks the equality offered by the kingdom of Communism. Quarreling within the church becomes a confused, obscure attempt to sway loyalties from one idolatrous kingdom to a different idolatrous kingdom. The process often involves a maximum of darkness, distrust and hostility rather than a maximum of light, clarity and love within the church. Strategy arguments come up for discussion within the church. People who are caught up in the pull for loyalty to one or the other secular kingdom do not realize the full scope of the discussion. Underlying a discussion of, for example, the motivational value of free enterprise versus the value of worker-controlled collectives is a demand for a choice between two idols or bent ideals. Two Christians can divide, choosing either freedom or equality, capitalism or communism, one idolatrous kingdom or the other. It is possible that they may not even realize they are being forced to choose between two secular realities and that God, in his wisdom, has proposed a third alternative.

The third alternative is a significant one. As this alternative relates to the United States, Christians are called to love our brothers and sisters in Christ, as well as even our enemies (Luke 6:32–36), as we love ourselves. We hear cries for liberation on the part of the people in Third World or developing countries. Often poverty, including lack of food, results in strife and armed conflicts. The debate arises as to whether citizens of the U.S. should better arm themselves to protect what they own while citizens of developing countries seek to tear down what they perceive to be prison bars that keep them out of trade systems and economic fairness. The fear exists that communism will establish a stronghold as it points toward the goal of equality. Not having other hope, people in need turn to communism and people with riches arm themselves or others with military weapons. Chaos results.

A value of God's system is that the rights of those in need are affirmed while those with power are called to lay down their lives and possessions voluntarily for those in need. Based on a relationship with God, the Christian is freed from personal concerns to love one's neighbor as oneself. Called to be content with food and clothing, Paul advises followers of Jesus to avoid the temptation of loving money. He goes on to exhort those who are rich to not hope in their goods but "to do good, to be rich in good deeds, liberal and generous . . ." (1 Timothy 6:8–18).

The followers of Jesus are admonished to have the mind of Christ. Not looking to only our own interests, we should consider others. We must follow Christ's example, who chose not to grasp equality with God but "emptied himself, taking the form of a servant . . ." (Philippians 2:4–11).

How is this ethic applied to world economic reality? From a Christian perspective, those in need should not be forced into a position where they feel they have no alternative but to break out of a prison of oppression. Rather, those Christians with resources have a responsibility to unlock the prison door and free the oppressed and the captives from the outside. The kingdom of God alternative is to preach good news to the poor. With Jesus, Christians are to proclaim release for the captives, recovery of sight to the blind, liberty for the oppressed, to proclaim the year of the Lord's favor (Luke 4:18–19). Through the voluntary sharing of personal resources, Christians in the United States have an opportunity to help declare the Gospel as the most viable economic alternative for setting the world in order.

If Christians define their economic theology in terms of either capitalism or communism, it is this secular materialist philosophy which will set the agenda for the church. People will decide to spend their lives succeeding in accumulating resources or enforcing redistribution of goods. The question is then raised as to how God fits into this agenda. In capitalism it produces quaint phrases such as "God helps those who help themselves" which is not in the Bible but sounds as though it ought to be. A cultural Christianity develops which encourages prosperity, abundance and a sense of God's judgment on those who fail to accumulate in this society. The verses on the slothful poor are emphasized while the overwhelming number of verses which refer to the poor as oppressed are ignored.[1] Selling possessions and giving to the poor are seen as admonitions for another time.

From a Marxist-Christian perspective, the Bible is interpreted to support the cause of the oppressed. However the liberation of the oppressed can become the all-important end point, justifying violence and the forced redistribution of goods. Paul's assertion that slaves ought to submit to their masters and call on God for justice ("revolutionary subordination" is the term John Howard Yoder uses[2]) is seen as an admonition for another time. One scholar even suggests that Jesus was killed before he could take the next step, "dealing with this oppressive force," the government of Rome.[3]

In both cases, Jesus' commandments become a means of justifying an economic system that the person is already committed to. Yet part of Jesus' mission was to point toward an economic order which is based not on material reality but spiritual reality where material goods serve a larger end.

Historical overview and analysis

A broad historical overview of the development of, and interplay among, the kingdoms of Capitalism, Communism and God begins with the suggestion that the church, up through the time of the Roman emperor Constantine, was voluntarily struggling to embody fairness, equality and justice. Christianity was a "fringe religion," attracting converts who were willing to forego social approval of a pagan culture and in some cases experience outright persecution. The struggle for equality and justice was met with varying degrees of success in the church from earliest times, as suggested, for example, in the New Testament Scripture.

With the official change in attitude which began with Constantine as early as 313 A.D., the social attitude toward the church changed as well. Beginning with merely stopping official persecution and providing Christian clergy the same rights as pagans, in the 5th century, pagans were commanded to " . . . go to the churches to receive Christian instruction, and exile and confiscation of property were made the penalties for refusing to be baptized." As a result of this state influence, "By the close of the first five centuries, Christianity had become the professed faith of the overwhelming majority of the population of the Roman Empire . . . . Many of the nominal Christians paid only lip service to their obstensible faith and remained pagans at heart. Yet outwardly Christianity had triumphed."[4]

To cope with the changing nature of the church, the sharing of material resources became less spontaneous and more organized. The church fathers continued to preach about the rigorous commitment to the call for justice which was integral to the Christian faith. Yet, only some remained open to the community lifestyle and sacrificial sharing which had been a necessary part of the early church. Many of those committed to such rigors joined monasteries. The bulk of the populace compromised with the dominant social system.

"The struggle to eradicate poverty as such ceased to exist, and was replaced by ways of alleviating the suffering of the poor . . . . This solution to the problem was to be decisive in the Church's response to the challenge of the poor and poverty in the centuries which followed. The intention was to relieve the suffering of the victims of injustice rather than to present a radical witness to the justice of God."[5]

The holy life, including works of charity, was a major emphasis of the monastic movement over the centuries to the time of the Reformation. At this time, the call to holiness was extended to and accepted by the laity in their everyday life. Max Weber details how the responsibility freely accepted in the monastic movement broadens out to large numbers of laypeople of the Reformation, thus beginning a partial reversal of the Constantinian synthesis.[6]

With that religious impulse in Protestant asceticism, the foundation of broad personal responsibility and initiative sets the stage for the emergence of secular capitalism which has survived to this day.

Given the extent of Christian influence in the culture, it is quite natural that the freedom, individual responsibility and initiative impulses evident in early Christianity should result in an economic system; while the other Christian impulse, equality, the neglected sibling, surfaces as a reaction to or even complement to secular capitalism in the form of secular communism. Both impulses exert their influence, now only partial reflections of the Christian perspective. It follows that these two secular cultural artifacts focusing on freedom or equality can be best understood as schizophrenic aspects of the original religious impulse embodied in the Reformation and the early church.

Capitalism in its classical form, focusing on individual freedom, initiative and responsibility is theoretically destroyed by state control. Its contemporary ideological support base has been linked with the assumption that a somewhat broadly diffused economic ownership in private hands helps to prevent concentration of power in the hands of the state thereby helping to ensure religious freedom.

Communism, with its need for strong centralized state control to implant equality within society, cannot afford immediate individualized freedom for all although, in theory, freedom is ultimately maximized for all.

In Christ, the believer is encouraged to work hard voluntarily as if working for God, while living for the other person with the fruits of one's enterprise, as though one were giving to God. In this way freedom and equality are theoretically maximized as fully integrated, rather than schizophrenically separated and yet locked into a matter/antimatter struggle of worldwide proportions.

As this struggle is played out on the brink of Armageddon, the pressure for resolution is increased by dwindling of renewable resources.

Jeremy Rifkin draws out the implications of this dynamic for the U.S. and secondarily for the church in the U.S. He says that only the church in the U.S. with its communication and general organizational network can tilt the U.S. away from a possible fascist attempt to consolidate its luxurious lifestyle, toward a more egalitarian attempt to seek justice on earth for all.[7]

As this drama has unfolded, a widespread phenomenon has emerged which the U.S. church has not yet integrated into its practical theology, the affluence of the past 40 years. For the first time in history the large majorities of people in a number of affluent nations no longer are spending all their resources or income to satisfy their basic requirements for food, shelter and clothing. Rather large portions of income are being expended to satisfy desires created through advertising.[8]

Therefore a great challenge lies before the church in the U.S. The church in the U.S. is large in numbers and exists in a nation which for the first time in history has massive resources in excess of those needed for meeting basic needs.

At one level, the challenge is to complete the religious impulse that manifested itself at the time of the Reformation. In addition to accepting the responsibility of working hard and living sacrificially on behalf of others, the church, rather than either accumulating or consuming wealth, must voluntarily redistribute it in Jesus' name in keeping with our Lord's clear command. We must transcend the Practical Theology of the Great Depression, emphasizing accumulation against past or future need which is such an integral part of American civil religion; we must seek to obey Jesus Christ the Lord of history.

As U. Milo Kaufmann in his book, *Heaven,* reflects:

"I think of the whole generation I have grown up with — those born in the Depression years of the 1930's. How diligently we have all scrambled, grasping at the opportunity for education and material advantage.

How quick to build comfortable homes with flower
gardens and great churches with five-acre parking
lots . . . . We lose the big picture, the big promise, God's
troubling call to the finest, in the fatness of the second
best."[9]

By sharing our wealth, we will be bridging the gap which
emerged at the time of the Constantinian synthesis. We will be
seeking broadbased justice as the whole Christian church, rather
than the alleviation of suffering accomplished by the ascetic-few
of the monastery.[10]

CHAPTER 15

The Light of the World

The choice before us

Part of God's plan is that he will never force himself on a person, although he is always available. In the initial turning from sin and death to life through Jesus as well as during the growing relationship between follower and Lord, the choice of pace and distance traveled in the relationship remains with the follower. The person has the choice whether s/he will be obedient to God and his ways.

That is why the choice before each individual Christian and the collective U.S. church is so critical. Each Christian can accept salvation, the promise of a happy forever, and live life in a business-as-usual fashion. The U.S. church can concern herself with internal affairs and remain concerned about world mission in a limited fashion. This type of religion has aptly been labeled "fire insurance."

The consequences of these actions, or lack of action, will not be evident until judgment. (Revelation 3:14–19, Matthew 25). Then the distractions of the world and the academic debates will be seen clearly as the robbers they are: the chance to serve God out of love in this earthly sojourn will be lost.

The individual salvation consequences of an undisciplined life are for formal theologians to debate. Whether one goes to Hell or merely goes to Heaven wishing one had done more for God will not be decided here.

It is clear, though, that thousands of our neighbors die daily, in pain, many without ever having heard about Jesus' love, while U.S. Christians have the resources to help them. It is also clear that God won't *make* us help them. If these overseas neighbors are helped by us, it will have to be because we want to help them.

Once we decide we want to do something, the choices before us are varied. In the previous pages, several suggestions have been offered. Those and other possible next steps are presented below.

Individual actions

In facing the task of world evangelism and poverty needs, the value of individual actions is very important. If you want to increase your involvement in meeting these needs, you can:

- Begin to pray daily for those in need, both at home and overseas in general.

- Look up what country your county is matched with in Appendix A and begin to pray for that country in particular.

- Do a Bible study on the topic of "the poor" by reading through the verses listed in your concordance.

- Find out about a local Christian outreach to the poor in your area and pray regularly for that outreach.

- Begin to volunteer in some capacity through your congregation or a local Christian ministry to the poor, being clear that you are hoping for personal contact with poor people.

- Ask your pastor for the names of missionaries or national church workers in the country with which your county is matched and begin to correspond with them.

- Make plans to increase your personal giving to 10 percent through your congregation, if you are not already doing so. Examine your lifestyle to see if you can increase giving beyond 10 percent if you are already giving at that level.

- Become involved in your congregational structure (mission committees, budget committees) to help increase a mission emphasis in your congregation.

- Study this book with other people in your congregation, including your pastor, with a goal toward seeing if there is sufficient interest in starting the journey toward becoming a "60-20-20" congregation.

— Help to coordinate educational events within your
congregation on stewardship, the potential of church
members in the U.S., need — both local and overseas
— particularly in the country with which your county
is matched. This may involve a variety of committees
including education, stewardship/budget, mission,
worship and music.

— Write your denominational headquarters, requesting
any material available on the country with which your
county is yoked; research that country in your local
library.

— Draft a proposal to be presented to your congregation
that it begin the process of becoming a 60-20-20 church.

Congregational actions

On the congregational level, there are a number of actions
that can be pursued. A stewardship or budget committee can
pursue these ideas through various means, including:

— Determine/estimate current per capita giving for your
congregation. Then compare your congregation expenditures with those in Table C for your congregation's
level of giving (see "Using Table C" for an explanation).

— Plan a theoretical budget, using the guidelines in Table
C, for your congregation at the 5 percent, 7 percent and
10 percent per capita giving levels. Present the congregation with these "dream" budgets.

— Provide educational classes that focus on need in your
area as well as overseas, with a particular emphasis on
the country with which your county is matched. Provide the congregation with denominational information
about what current activities are going on in that
country.

— Contact other congregations in your area, either of the
same denomination or of different denominations.

Explore the possibility of a common missions fair with a focus on the area with which your county is matched.

— If your congregation can provide ways for members to have personal contact with the local poor, publicize these activities. If the congregation is not currently involved in such outreach, explore what ministries to the poor exist in your local area.

— Contact your denomination to explore the possibility of a more personal relationship with Christians in the country with which you are yoked.

— Contact your denomination regarding:

a. the possibility of national church leaders from the country you are yoked with visiting your congregation, or a meeting of congregations, in your area when such national church leaders are in the U.S.

b. being placed on a mailing list of updated church materials related to the country with which you are matched.

c. the existence or possibility of a translation service to facilitate communication with church leaders in the country with which you are matched.

d. whether the congregation can designate funds for a given country and receive feedback as to how those funds are used.

e. what percentage of your congregation's proposed increase in mission funds would be used for overhead within the U.S. and what percentage would be used in the country with which your county is yoked.

A city on a hill

That God wants to extend Jesus' love and caring to all residents of the world should be evident. That the U.S. church, individually and collectively, has great resources, should also be clear. One point that needs to be reemphasized is that God also has joy and blessing for his follower who chooses to assist others in Jesus' name.

Promises abound for the Christian who chooses, out of love, to value others. "Seek ye first the kingdom of God, and his righteousness; and all these things shall be added unto you" (Matthew 6:33 KJV).

It appears that, while God calls us to a life of obedient servanthood, he does not do it out of hostility or meanness, but out of love for us and a hope that our joy will be fulfilled. The God who asks us to serve others asked the same of his own Son. This God who asks us to share with others counts the very hairs on our heads, thus evidencing his care for us.

Christians in the U.S. must decide what to do with the abundant resources at our disposal. The decision must be made Christian by Christian, individual by individual. One need not wait for the whole congregation to seek out cross-cultural opportunities, to educate oneself through the Yoking Map or to share 10 percent of one's income.

To the degree, however, that such discipleship does not remain on the individual level but reaches out through the whole congregation, the denomination and to brothers and sisters in Christ overseas, to that degree we can rejoice in Jesus telling us in Matthew 5:14-16:

> *You are the light of the world. A city set on a hill cannot be hid. Nor do men light a lamp and put it under a bushel, but on a stand, and it gives light to all in the house. Let your light so shine before men, that they may see your good works and give glory to your Father who is in heaven.*

What an exciting way to spend one's life. What a glorious vision. As always, the choice remains ours: how far will we let the Light shine.

NOTES

Chapter 1

1. *Food Policy Issues for the Eighth Session: Report by the Executive Director* (New York: United Nations World Food Council, March 12, 1982), p. 6.

Chapter 4

1. Randall Wayne Schertz, *An Analysis of the Land Tenure System in Pernambuco, Brazil: A Case for Land Reform,* (Master's Thesis, Urbana-Champaign: University of Illinois, 1974), p. 82.

2. *Ibid.,* p. 15.

Chapter 6

1. Donald McGavran, *Lausanne Occasional Papers, No. 1. The Pasadena Consultation — Homogeneous Unit* (Wheaton, Illinois: Lausanne Committee for World Evangelism, 1978), p. 3.

2. Jim Hamaan, "One City One Church," *New Wine,* February, 1974, p. 27.

3. *World Christian Encyclopedia,* David B. Barrett, ed. (New York: Oxford University Press, 1982), p. 4.

Chapter 7

1. "On Being Stretched Between Two Poles," *MARC Newsletter,* World Vision, March, 1976, p. 5.

2. Harvey T. Hoekstra, *The World Council of Churches and the Demise of Evangelism* (Wheaton, Illinois: Tyndale, 1979), pp. 16–17.

3. Walbert Bühlman, "Mission in the 1980's: Two Viewpoints," *Occasional Bulletin of Missionary Research,* Vol. 4, No. 3. July, 1980, p. 98.

4. Emilio Castro, "Mission Today and Tomorrow: A Conversation," *International Bulletin of Missionary Research,* July, 1981, p. 111.

5. *The African Food Problem and the Role of International Agencies: Report by the Executive Director,* (New York: United Nations World Food Council, February 22, 1982), pp. 5–6.

6. Robert S. McNamara, *Address to the Board of Governors,* International Bank for Reconstruction and Development, Washington, October 4, 1976, p. 14.

7. Shavid Javed Burki, "Sectoral Priorities for Meeting Basic Needs," *Finance and Development,* International Monetary Fund and International Bank for Reconstruction and Development, Washington, D.C., Vol. 17, No. 1, March, 1980, p. 20.

8. *Ibid.* p. 22.

9. Lester R. Brown and Gail Finsterbusch, *Man and His Environment: Food* (New York: Harper and Row, 1972), p. 142.

10. Frances Moore Lappé and Joseph Collins, with Cary Fowler. *Food First: Beyond the Myth of Scarcity,* Revised (New York: Ballantine Books, 1978), pp. 392–393.

Chapter 8

1. C. Hugo Zorilla, "The Same Dog with a Different Chain?" *Gospel Herald,* Vol. 70, No. 40, October 11, 1977, p. 759.

2. Frederick Wilson, "Beyond the Empty Slogans," *AD Magazine,* October 1981, p. 20.

3. The specific deed/word ratio of 10:1 is based on empirical considerations as follows. Using 1979 Christian giving potential of around $95 billion at the 10 percent average per capita level of giving, we would have had slightly over $55 billion in additional funds for global mission if we used the 58.7 percent allocation suggested in Table C. *The Report of the Independent Commission on International Development Issues* under the Chairmanship of Willy Brandt, (Cambridge: MIT Press, 1980), p. 241, notes in a discussion of possible global development needs, "Suggestions for 'massive transfers' have ranged from $10 to $50 billion per year." Without necessarily embracing all of the assumptions of development outlined in the Brandt Report, adoption of the upper range estimate of $50 billion for global deed missions would mean allocating $5 billion for overseas word mission.

Corresponding to a hoped for minimum 500 percent increase in average individual giving from the 1.6 percent level to the 10 percent level, the $5 billion for overseas word mission amounts to approximately a 500 percent increase in word missions funding over the current level if we assume that 50 percent of all current overseas mission giving is used for word missions. This very rough estimate of the portion of the total U.S. church's mission budget currently used for word missions is partly based on a perusal of the "Types of Ministries" section of *Mission Handbook*, (Monrovia: MARC, 1980), pp. 22, 64–66. A general estimate of $750 million for word missions in 1979 is adopted.

In this consideration of word and deed missions, it remains for us to make explicit a working definition of word and deed missions. By word missions, reference is made to activities such as church planting/establishing, personal and small group evangelism, mass evangelism, literature distribution, etc. Categories such as development, aid/relief, childcare, medical care, agricultural assistance, etc., are included in, but do not exhaust, the designation deed mission.

Clearly, there is overlap between word mission and deed mission in many situations. That the task of neatly categorizing the mission world into word and deed categories is difficult, if not impossible, is highlighted by the fact that the *Mission Handbook,* pp. 67–117 in a section entitled "Agencies Listed by Primary Task" has a listing of 119 primary tasks. Nevertheless, as we think of increasing the total mission budget some 3000 percent from $1.8 billion to $55 billion, it is of some help to consider a general direction by suggesting overall budgetary goals for the word and deed mission categories. This is particularly the case insofar as within the U.S. church, some emphasize word missions over against deed mission and vice versa, while according to an examination of current church finances, neither grouping is living anywhere near sacrificially on behalf of those in great need overseas.

For further discussion see Appendix B.

4. In the area of deed mission, certain words seem to indicate particular theories about addressing solutions for problems confronting the Third World. "Development" tends to indicate specific assumptions about economic needs in Third World countries — as the economy develops and new trade markets and industries grow, people's lives will improve. Another approach is summed up by the term "liberation." In this approach to deed mission, it is assumed that the current international economic system is unfair and often, the economic system within a nation is unfair. Therefore, people need to be liberated from an unjust situation. A term currently surfacing in regard to deed mission is "social transformation." According to this approach, assuming that the current Third World situation is in need of change, a social transformation, employing Biblical principles, should be pursued to create a new, perhaps as yet unknown system, which may also require change in the rest of the world.

Chapter 9

1. In fact, there is some debate on whether the ethics of Jesus apply to 20th century Christianity. An interesting defense of the relevance of Jesus' ethics to today appears in John Howard Yoder's *The Politics of Jesus* (Grand Rapids: William B. Eerdmans Publishing Co., 1980), Chapter 1.

2. C. Peter Wagner and Edward R. Dayton, ed., *Unreached Peoples '80,* (Elgin: David C. Cook Publishing Co., 1980), p. 8.

3. *World Christian Encyclopedia,* David B. Barrett, ed. (New York: Oxford University Press, 1982), p. 3.

4. Jeremy Rifkin with Ted Howard, *The Emerging Order: God in an Age of Scarcity* (New York: G.P. Putnam's Sons, 1979), p. 58.

5. *MARC Newsletter,* World Vision, September 1979, p. 1.

6. *MARC Newsletter,* World Vision, November, 1973, pp. 4–5; *World Vision Magazine,* May 1978, p. 3.

7. *The United Methodist Reporter,* The Messenger Edition, September 4, 1981, p. 5.

8. Lester R. Brown and Gail W. Finsterbusch, *Man and His Environment: Food* (New York: Harper and Row, 1972), p. 14; W. Stanley Mooneyham, *What Do You Say to a Hungry World?* (Waco: Word, 1975), p. 27.

9. James P. Grant, *The State of the World's Children, 1982–83,* (New York: United Nations, 1983), p. 1.

10. *Report of the World Food Council on the Work of Its Fifth Session,* (New York: United Nations, 1979), p. 9.

11. *Implementation of the "Manila Communique of the World Food Council:" . . . Report by the Executive Director* (WFC/1978/5), (New York: United Nations World Food Council, April 17, 1978), p. 16.

12. *World Press Review,* January 1, 1980, p. 56.

13. Alan Berg, *The Nutritional Factor: Its Role in Nutritional Development* (Washington D.C.: The Brookings Institute, 1973), pp. 3–4.

14. Willy Brandt, *North-South, A Program for Survival* (Cambridge: MIT Press, 1980), p. 241.

15. James P. Grant, pp. 2, 11.

16. Ruth Leger Sivard, *World Military and Social Expenditures* (Leesburg, Virginia: World Priorities, 1981), p. 23.

Chapter 10

1. See footnote 3, (paragraph 3 below).

2. Willy Brandt, *North-South, A Program for Survival,* (Cambridge: MIT Press, 1980), p. 241. The figures noted have been updated to 1983 dollars.

3. The estimate we have derived for the percent of adherent per capita giving by individual living donors through Christian congregations is 1.6 percent. Four assumptions upon which this estimate is based deserve mention: a) 50 percent of the U.S. population constitute the adherent giving base for Christian congregations; b) about 90 percent of all individual religious giving in the U.S. was given to Christian organizations and agencies (based on our adjustment of Christian population omitting Marginal Protestants, *World Christian Encyclopedia, op. cit.,* p. 711); c) 10 percent of all Christian giving may be estimated to be contributed through Christian paradenominational agencies other than congregations; and d) 5 percent of all Christian giving may be estimated to have been given by bequests, foundations and corporations (based primarily on an estimate that of the 6 percent of total contributions donated through bequests noted in the *Church Financial Statistics and Related Data 1981,* (New York: National Council of Churches), p. 8, somewhat less than half was given to Christian congre-

gations, denominations and interdenominational and paradenominational organizations). Therefore the paradenominational, and bequest, foundation and corporate gifts are
subtracted from the Christian giving noted in point b) above to
determine the amount given by individual adherent living
Christian donors through congregations.

The entries in Table A were derived from the Total 1980
Dollar Amounts Available at the 1.6 percent level of giving which
is assumed to approximate the current level of giving. The dollar
estimate at the 1.6 percent level of giving is in turn based on the
above assumptions. Specific values used in obtaining this dollar
estimate, and their respective sources are as follows. a) U.S.
1980 population was 227,171,590. This population estimate
was obtained by dividing total personal income by per capita
personal income as found in *Survey of Current Business,* April
1982, Vol. 62, Number 4, Bureau of Economics, U.S. Department of Commerce, Table 1, p. 51 and matches the estimate of
227.2 millions resident population presented in Table 2 of the
Statistical Abstract of the United States, Bureau of Census, U.S.
Department of Commerce, 1981, p. 5. b) Religious giving in the
U.S. in 1980 was $22.15 billion according to *Giving U.S.A.:*
1981 Annual Report, American Association of Fund-Raising
Counsel, Inc., 1981, p. 6. c) *The World Christian Encyclopedia,*
Oxford University Press, 1982, p. 711 indicates that 90.7 percent of the U.S. religious population is Christian, excluding the
category Marginal Protestants. d) U.S. 1980 per capita personal
income was $9511, *Survey of Current Business, op. cit.*

The actual Table entries are midyear 1983 data derived from
the United States Total Personal Income estimate as found in
"Current Business Statistics," *Survey of Current Business,*
Bureau of Economic Analysis of the U.S. Department of
Commerce, August 1983, p. S-1. Thus the assumed giving
amount at the 1.6 percent level is a projection derived from 1980
based data and expressed in this Table in midyear 1983 dollars
on the basis of midyear 1983 Total Personal Income.

4. *U.S. News and World Report,* August 10, 1981, pp. 61–
63.

5. The 42 denominations selected were those listed in the *Yearbook of American and Canadian Churches 1982,* Constant H. Jacquet Jr., ed., (Nashville: Abingdon), in addition to the Free Methodist Church of North America and the Assemblies of God, data for which was drawn from the 1980 and 1975 editions of the *Yearbook,* respectively.

6. Per capita adherent contributions expressed as a percentage of per capita income were obtained as follows. The percentages in this column, which were rounded to the nearest tenth of a percent, were obtained simply by dividing "Per Capita Inclusive Membership Total Contributions" as listed in the *Yearbook* by per capita income as presented in the *Survey of Current Business,* April, 1982, p. 53 ($9511 for 1980; $8638 for 1979) and April, 1983, p. 41 ($10,495 for 1981). In the case of the Free Methodist and the Assembly of God denominations, per capita personal income was obtained from the *Statistical Abstract of the United States 1981,* p. 423 for the years 1978 and 1974 respectively.

Twenty-two of the denominations had the same (or nearly the same in the case of the Church of the Nazarene) full and inclusive membership estimates in the *Yearbook.* In the two instances, Church of the Lutheran Confession and Evangelical Mennonite Brethren Conference, in which Inclusive Membership in the *Yearbook* was higher than the corresponding figure for Total Adherents in *Churches and Church Membership in the United States 1980,* Bernard Quinn, Herman Anderson, Martin Bradley, Paul Goetting, and Peggy Shriver, (Atlanta: Glenmary Research Center, 1982), pp. 1–2, the *Yearbook* figures were used without any adjustments. This situation also obtained with regard to The Schwenkfelder Church with a comparison of *Yearbook* and *World Christian Encyclopedia* data (p. 724). For the remaining nineteen denominations, the percentages derived as described in the above paragraph were adjusted as follows. The percentages (in decimal form to the tenth place) for eighteen denominations were multiplied by the ratio of communicant, confirmed, full members to total adherents as listed in *Churches and Church Membership in the United States*

1980, pp. 1-3. The ratio of Communicant, Confirmed, Full Members to Total Adherents for the General Association of General Baptists was obtained from *Churches and Church Membership in the United States 1971,* Douglas W. Johnson, Paul R. Ricard, and Peggy Shriver (Washington D.C.: Glenmary Research Center, 1974), p. 1. Since this above-mentioned ratio in *Churches and Church Membership in the United States 1980* was 1.00 for the Evangelical Church of North America, the above-mentioned procedure had no effect on the *Yearbook* figures for this denomination.

7. This column was obtained by multiplying the Total Column by the Percentage of Contributions Available for Benevolences as Actually Used According to Specific Denomination Data, refigured to the nearest hundredth of a percent. The results were rounded to the nearest hundredth of a percent.

8. The domestic and global benevolence allocations at the 2.5 percent levels of giving and below (2, 1.6 and 1 in this Table) are based on a broad scale estimate that approximately 5 percent of the giving through congregations was used for overseas word and deed mission. Let us further assume that the total church mission budget is comprised of two more or less equal amounts from denominational (including congregational and denominationally-constituted interdenominational sources) and paradenominational sources.

Although sufficient information is perhaps not available to provide a precise evaluation of these estimates, pursuit of the matter might take note of the following observations: a) 5 percent of congregational giving (including Protestant, Roman Catholic and Orthodox) in 1979 amounted to roughly $750 million; b) an equal amount of overseas mission from paradenominational sources would yield a total mission budget of about $1.5 billion which in turn is approximately 10 percent of the amount estimated to have been contributed through congregational sources in 1979. If we assume, as was suggested in Note 3, Chapter 10, that paradenominational giving is 10 percent of all Christian giving, it follows that in 1979 with a total Christian giving of approximately $18 billion, global mission and domestic allocations would have constituted about 42 and 57 percent of total paradenominational income respectively; c) U.S. Protestant mission agencies including denominational agencies reported a total 1979 cash income for overseas ministries of approximately $1.1 billion (*Mission Handbook, op. cit.*, p. 56, 61); d) a small sampling of the percent of selected denominational total contributions spent on overseas mission found some large denominations below 5 percent ("Mission Agencies", *Mission Handbook*, pp. 137–509 and *Church Financial Statistics and Related Data 1980*, p. 4).

9. John Perkins, "Bicentennial in the Other America," *Sojourners*, January, 1976, p. 23.

10. Mark Hatfield, "Statement on Senate Bill 2502," *Congressional Record*, Vol. 119, Part 25, October 1, 1973, p. 32157.

11. This estimate of 260 active adherents per congregation with income above poverty level is based on the following assumptions and information. Approximately half of the U.S. population, that is, about 114.67 million in 1982, is estimated as consisting of church adherents actively involved in their congregations. With a 1982 poverty rate of 15.0 percent, of these adherents, 17,200,500 are estimated as having had income below poverty level (Census Bureau estimates of 1982 U.S. population and percent below poverty, were respectively derived and obtained directly from *The New York Times*, August 2, 1983, p. 1). This leaves 97,469,500 active adherents with income above poverty level. In 1982, these adherents organized into about 370,000 congregations, not counting approximately 20,000 congregations of Marginal Protestants. (*World Christian Encyclopedia, op cit.*, pp. 720–725).

12. There were 34.4 million persons below poverty level in 1982 (*The New York Times, op cit.*) and, as stated in note 11 above, there were approximately 370,000 congregations.

13. In looking at church potential for sharing within the U.S., it is of interest to examine the possibilities of Christians sharing their income. Consider, for example, the goal of two times poverty level income for each household in the U.S. For purposes of discussion, it is suggested here that, on the average, somewhere around a gross income equal to two times poverty level is required to live at a somewhat reasonable level within the contemporary U.S.

Using our earlier assumption that half of the U.S. population are active church adherents, then we note that in 1981 there is approximately one church person with income above two times poverty level for each person below two times poverty level. However, the income possessed by those church adherents above two times poverty level is approximately $830 billion while the corresponding aggregate cash income of all those with income below two times poverty level is about $245 billion. If through their churches, richer Christians voluntarily shared sufficient funds such that all those below two times poverty level had income at the two times poverty level, and if these same Christians limited their living expenditures to the two times poverty level, there would be a remainder of $230 billion. This $230 billion would be available to cover the higher income and social security taxes incurred by those Christians with incomes above two times poverty level, the higher housing costs those churched folk with income higher than two times poverty level might initially have, additional savings, additional education and retirement costs, and increased giving.

The 1981 Aggregate Income Deficit, that is, the total amount by which the total cash income of those below poverty level falls below poverty level was $37 billion. This figure does not take into consideration the market value of means-tested noncash benefits which were estimated to be about $72.5 billion in 1980. The above information was derived for the most part from the following sources: U.S. Bureau of Census, *Current Population Reports,* Series P-60, Nos. 136–138, entitled "Characteristics of Households and Persons Receiving Selected

Noncash Benefits: 1981," "Money Income of Households, Families, and Persons in the United States: 1981," and "Characteristics of the Population Below the Poverty Level: 1981," respectively, U.S. Government Printing Office, Washington, D.C., 1983.

14. *Statistical Abstract of the United States, 1981*, U.S. Census Bureau, Washington, D.C., GPO, p. 423 and *Church Financial Statistics and Related Data, 1981, op. cit.*, p. 18.

15. Ruth Leger Sivard, *World Military and Social Expenditures, 1983* (Washington, D.C.: World Priorities, 1983), p. 33.

16. *Voluntary Foreign Aid Program, 1981, Bureau for Food for Peace and Voluntary Assistance*, Agency for International Development, Department of State, Washington, D.C., pp. 3, 21.

17. Many thinkers stress the importance of the growth of Third World economies for the continued well-being of the industrialized economies. Some futurists emphasize the need to capitalize a steady-state economy in a post-industrialized society. To proceed in following Jesus along the lines suggested does not require a prior commitment to any single economic scenario for the future.

18. Aspects of this idea are explored by Doris Donnelly in "The Needle's Eye: Christians and their Money," *The Christian Century*, April 27, 1983, pp. 400–402, and Douglas John Hall in *The Steward: A Biblical Symbol Come of Age*, (New York: Friendship Press, 1982).

Chapter 11

1. James P. Grant, *The State of the World's Children 1981–82,* United Nations, New York, December, 1981, p. 10.

2. Willy Brandt, *North-South, A Program for Survival,* (Cambridge: MIT Press, 1980), p. 16.

3. J. K. Galbraith, *The Affluent Society* (New York: New American Library, Third Edition Revised, 1976), p. 233, and *The New Industrial State* (New York: New American Library, Third Edition, Revised, 1978), pp. 33–34, 193, 289.

4. C. S. Lewis, *The Weight of Glory and Other Addresses* (Grand Rapids: Eerdmans Publishers, 1966), pp. 14–15.

5. James P. Grant, *The State of the World's Children 1982–83,* United Nations, New York, 1983, p. 7.

6. University of Illinois Conference, "Understanding the World Food System: Its Importance to Illinois," Urbana, Illinois, February 14–15, 1982.

7. Mahbub ul Haq, "An International Perspective on Basic Needs," *Finance and Development,* September, 1980, p. 13.

8. Francis Moore Lappé and Joseph Collins, *Food First, Beyond the Myth of Scarcity* (New York: Ballentine Books, 1978), p. 39.

Chapter 12

1. *Mission Handbook: North American Protestant Ministries Overseas,* Samuel Wilson, ed. (Monrovia, California: MARC, 1980), p. 46, 547–702.

2. *Selections from the Writings of John Wesley,* Herbert Welch, ed., (Nashville: Abingdon Press, 1942), p. 208.

3. *Ibid.*

Chapter 13

1. At this point it may be good to consider areas which are of concern to the populace at large within the U.S. Generally speaking, in the U.S., the popular concern is in defending Christian capitalism with its focus on freedom, particularly as manifest against the East's godless communism with its focus on equality as embodied in the U.S.S.R.

The fact that there is perceived by the U.S. a general communist identity which has threatening elements can be documented from the popular press. A November, 1980 *Reader's Digest* article mentions "Cuba's Fidel Castro strives to export communism throughout the region" (p. 128). *U.S. News and World Report* asked on its December 21, 1981 cover "Is Central America Going Communist?" and on March 1, 1982, its cover banner is the general indictment, "Communism, The Great Economic Failure."

Although equality and freedom may or may not be better integrated in some forms of democratic socialism implemented in, for example, Sweden or the United Kingdom, the question of democratic socialism is not a high visibility issue in the U.S. and thus will not occupy our attention here. Further the conviction expressed in this chapter is that the primary issue for U.S. Christians is obedience to Jesus Christ with the resources we possess. As this is done, we will more clearly see whatever other complementary steps should be taken in the public arena. Our first concern must be loyalty to the kingdom of God without prejudging what economic system might or might not develop.

2. *World Population Data Sheet,* Population Reference Bureau, Inc., Washington, D.C., 1980.

3. Dom Helder Camara, *Revolution Through Peace,* translated from the Portuguese by Amparo McLean (New York: Harper and Row, 1981), p. 58.

4. Buckminster Fuller, *Critical Path* (New York: St. Martin's Press, 1981), pp. 196–97.

Chapter 14

1. Tom Hanks, "Why People Are Poor," *Sojourners,* January, 1981, pp. 19–22.

2. John Howard Yoder, *The Politics of Jesus* (Grand Rapids: William B. Eerdmans Publishing Company, 7th printing, 1980), Chapter 9.

3. George V. Pixley, *God's Kingdom, A Guide for Biblical Study* (Maryknoll: Orbis Books, 1977), pp. 76–77.

4. Kenneth Scott Latourette, *A History of Christianity* (New York: Harper, 1953), pp. 97–98.

5. Julio de Santa Ana, *Good News to the Poor* (Maryknoll: Orbis Books, 1979), pp. 77–78.

6. Max Weber, *The Protestant Ethic and the Spirit of Capitalism* (New York: Scribners, 1958 edition).

7. Jeremy Rifkin, *The Emerging Order: God in the Age of Scarcity* (New York: G.P. Putnam and Sons, 1979).

8. John Kenneth Galbraith, *The New Industrial State* (New York: New American Library, Third Edition, Revised, 1978), pp. 33–34, 193, 289.

9. U. Milo Kaufmann, *Heaven* (Winona Lake, Indiana: Light and Life Press, 1981), p. 53.

10. John Howard Yoder lays an excellent scholarly foundation for this needed movement within the U.S. church with his *The Politics of Jesus, op. cit.,* which demonstrates the necessary applicability of the Messianic ethic in our time as well as in the time of the early church.

APPENDIX A

Yoking Map

U.S. Counties, U.S. Church Resources Available for Global Word and Deed Mission at the 10 Percent Giving Level Using the 60-20-20 Distribution Formula, and Nations with Which U.S. Counties Are Matched[1]

U.S. County	U.S. Church Resources Available for Global Word and Deed Mission (Dollars)	Nation	U.S. County	U.S. Church Resources Available for Global Word and Deed Mission (Dollars)	Nation
Alabama	$ 1,265,274,000		Marshall	21,694,000	India
Autauga	8,498,000	India	Mobile	117,204,000	India
Baldwin	22,805,000	India	Monroe	7,129,000	India
Barbour	5,561,000	India	Montgomery	74,675,000	India
Bibb	3,880,000	India	Morgan	33,399,000	India
Blount	8,674,000	India	Perry	2,559,000	India
Bullock	3,005,000	India	Pickens	6,333,000	India
Butler	9,124,000	India	Pike	6,630,000	India
Calhoun	37,223,000	India	Randolph	5,540,000	India
Chambers	11,732,000	India	Russell	11,380,000	India
Cherokee	5,602,000	India	St. Clair	10,913,000	India
Chilton	9,357,000	India	Shelby	14,636,000	India
Choctaw	5,038,000	India	Sumter	3,331,000	India
Clarke	8,908,000	India	Talladega	21,152,000	India
Clay	4,748,000	India	Tallapoosa	12,248,000	India
Cleburne	4,054,000	India	Tuscaloosa	38,196,000	India
Coffee	13,608,000	India	Walker	24,543,000	India
Colbert	19,366,000	India	Washington	5,355,000	India
Conecuh	4,636,000	India	Wilcox	2,203,000	India
Coosa	2,761,000	India	Winston	7,113,000	India
Covington	12,255,000	India			
Crenshaw	4,070,000	India	Alaska[2]	$ 106,796,000	
Cullman	22,632,000	India	Aleutian Islands	1,360,000	U.S.S.R.
Dale	9,981,000	India	Anchorage	47,837,000	U.S.S.R.
Dallas	10,501,000	India	Bethel	2,785,000	U.S.S.R.
De Kalb	12,604,000	India	Bristol Bay	158,000	U.S.S.R.
Elmore	13,822,000	India	Dillingham	785,000	U.S.S.R.
Escambia	9,571,000	India	Fairbanks North Star	12,839,000	U.S.S.R.
Etowah	39,078,000	India	Haines	367,000	U.S.S.R.
Fayette	5,773,000	India	Juneau	8,054,000	U.S.S.R.
Franklin	7,480,000	India	Kenai Peninsula	4,956,000	U.S.S.R.
Geneva	8,157,000	India	Ketchikan Gateway	4,640,000	U.S.S.R.
Greene	2,194,000	India	Kobuk	1,818,000	U.S.S.R.
Hale	3,106,000	India	Kodiak Island	1,479,000	U.S.S.R.
Henry	3,659,000	India	Matanuska-Susitna	3,163,000	U.S.S.R.
Houston	25,489,000	India	Nome	1,700,000	U.S.S.R.
Jackson	12,479,000	India	North Slope	1,528,000	U.S.S.R.
Jefferson	287,560,000	India	Prince of Wales-		
Lamar	4,523,000	India	Out Ketchikan	565,000	U.S.S.R.
Lauderdale	26,785,000	India	Sitka	2,853,000	U.S.S.R.
Lawrence	6,409,000	India	Skagway-Yakutat-		
Lee	24,919,000	India	Angoon	656,000	U.S.S.R.
Limestone	12,542,000	India	Southeast Fairbanks	605,000	U.S.S.R.
Lowndes	2,606,000	India	Valdez-Cordova	3,419,000	U.S.S.R.
Macon	1,933,000	India	Wade Hampton	1,134,000	U.S.S.R.
Madison	67,147,000	India	Wrangell-Petersburg	1,541,000	U.S.S.R.
Marengo	7,134,000	India	Yukon-Koyukuk	2,554,000	U.S.S.R.
Marion	6,052,000	India			

U.S. County	U.S. Church Resources Available for Global Word and Deed Mission (Dollars)	Nation
Arizona	$ 622,752,000	
Apache	5,060,000	Thailand
Cochise	15,880,000	Thailand
Coconino	13,497,000	Thailand
Gila	11,007,000	Thailand
Graham	4,408,000	Thailand
Greenlee	5,566,000	Thailand
Maricopa	146,940,000	Kampuchea
	86,312,000	Laos
	129,869,000	Thailand
Mohave	9,448,000	Laos
Navajo	7,967,000	Thailand
Pima	126,571,000	Thailand
Pinal	21,368,000	Thailand
Santa Cruz	6,131,000	Thailand
Yavapai	16,449,000	Laos
Yuma	16,279,000	Kampuchea
Arkansas	$ 707,518,000	
Arkansas	9,336,000	China
Ashley	9,065,000	China
Baxter	7,625,000	China
Benton	22,899,000	China
Boone	8,151,000	China
Bradley	4,005,000	China
Calhoun	1,321,000	China
Carroll	3,439,000	China
Chicot	2,554,000	China
Clark	7,124,000	China
Clay	5,419,000	China
Cleburne	3,780,000	China
Cleveland	2,080,000	China
Columbia	9,800,000	China
Conway	4,904,000	China
Craighead	23,257,000	China
Crawford	8,041,000	China
Crittenden	9,815,000	China
Cross	6,438,000	China
Dallas	2,974,000	China
Desha	4,600,000	China
Drew	4,294,000	China
Faulkner	12,469,000	China
Franklin	3,532,000	China
Fulton	1,923,000	China
Garland	24,872,000	China
Grant	4,438,000	China
Greene	10,307,000	China
Hempstead	9,435,000	China
Hot Spring	8,569,000	China
Howard	7,210,000	China
Independence	9,295,000	China
Izard	3,308,000	China
Jackson	5,909,000	China
Jefferson	25,230,000	China
Johnson	3,993,000	China
Lafayette	2,700,000	China
Lawrence	5,340,000	China
Lee	2,038,000	China
Lincoln	2,138,000	China
Little River	4,008,000	China
Logan	6,046,000	China
Lonoke	11,517,000	China
Madison	1,462,000	China
Marion	2,105,000	China
Miller	12,887,000	China
Mississippi	17,416,000	China
Monroe	3,238,000	China
Montgomery	1,438,000	China
Nevada	3,466,000	China
Newton	552,000	China
Ouachita	10,377,000	China
Perry	1,696,000	China
Phillips	6,695,000	China
Pike	2,580,000	China
Poinsett	8,716,000	China
Polk	4,839,000	China
Pope	8,975,000	China
Prairie	2,694,000	China
Pulaski	138,587,000	China
Randolph	3,703,000	China
St. Francis	7,530,000	China
Saline	14,193,000	China
Scott	2,115,000	China
Searcy	1,093,000	China
Sebastian	45,808,000	China
Sevier	3,870,000	China
Sharp	3,850,000	China
Stone	1,433,000	China
Union	21,336,000	China
Van Buren	2,693,000	China
Washington	24,382,000	China
White	15,835,000	China
Woodruff	2,913,000	China
Yell	3,843,000	China
California	$ 6,421,581,000	
Alameda	327,161,000	Indonesia
Alpine	38,000	East Timor
Amador	3,512,000	East Timor
Butte	20,335,000	Philippines
Calaveras	3,065,000	East Timor
Colusa	4,049,000	Philippines
Contra Costa	212,506,000	Indonesia
Del Norte	4,014,000	Philippines
El Dorado	9,644,000	Philippines
Fresno	142,795,000	Indonesia
Glenn	6,808,000	Philippines
Humboldt	21,491,000	Philippines
Imperial	32,761,000	Kampuchea
Inyo	5,458,000	Vietnam
Kern	107,098,000	Indonesia
Kings	17,654,000	Indonesia
Lake	5,296,000	Philippines
Lassen	2,405,000	Philippines
Los Angeles	1,920,172,000	Indonesia
	503,577,000	Vietnam
Madera	14,164,000	Indonesia
Marin	68,474,000	Philippines
Mariposa	1,152,000	East Timor
Mendocino	10,327,000	Philippines
Merced	8,928,000	East Timor
	32,325,000	Indonesia
Modoc	1,156,000	Philippines
Mono	292,000	Vietnam
Monterey	65,438,000	Indonesia
Napa	26,855,000	Philippines
Nevada	5,402,000	Philippines
Orange	542,000	Brunei
	169,510,000	Malaysia
	5,148,000	Singapore
Placer	346,029,000	Vietnam
Plumas	19,821,000	Philippines
Riverside	2,603,000	Philippines
Sacramento	128,710,000	Vietnam
San Benito	172,009,000	Philippines
San Bernardino	4,096,000	Indonesia
San Diego	187,468,000	Vietnam
	11,632,000	Kampuchea
	382,882,000	Vietnam
San Francisco	205,275,000	Philippines
San Joaquin	98,505,000	Indonesia
San Luis Obispo	27,550,000	Indonesia
San Mateo	171,487,000	Indonesia
	37,074,000	Philippines
Santa Barbara	82,028,000	Indonesia
Santa Clara	316,338,000	Indonesia

U.S. County	U.S. Church Resources Available for Global Word and Deed Mission (Dollars)	Nation
Santa Cruz	34,930,000	Indonesia
Shasta	15,757,000	Philippines
Sierra	487,000	Philippines
Siskiyou	7,890,000	Philippines
Solano	46,343,000	Philippines
Sonoma	59,524,000	Philippines
Stanislaus	59,455,000	Indonesia
Sutter	10,828,000	Philippines
Tehama	5,702,000	Philippines
Trinity	642,000	Philippines
Tulare	62,441,000	Indonesia
Tuolumne	3,982,000	East Timor
Ventura	128,895,000	Indonesia
Yolo	24,779,000	Philippines
Yuba	6,867,000	Philippines
Colorado	$ 759,911,000	
Adams	51,909,000	China
Alamosa	3,942,000	China
Arapahoe	74,821,000	China
Archuleta	1,246,000	China
Baca	992,000	China
Bent	2,207,000	China
Boulder	50,772,000	China
Chaffee	3,910,000	China
Cheyenne	887,000	China
Clear Creek	670,000	China
Conejos	1,378,000	China
Costilla	1,150,000	China
Crowley	945,000	China
Custer	309,000	China
Delta	4,048,000	China
Denver	189,995,000	China
Dolores	250,000	China
Douglas	4,914,000	China
Eagle	1,315,000	China
Elbert	735,000	China
El Paso	66,410,000	China
Fremont	6,144,000	China
Garfield	5,689,000	China
Gilpin	94,000	China
Grand	927,000	China
Gunnison	951,000	China
Hinsdale	32,000	China
Huerfano	1,193,000	China
Jackson	241,000	China
Jefferson	86,282,000	China
Kiowa	454,000	China
Kit Carson	3,395,000	China
Lake	2,903,000	China
La Plata	4,687,000	China
Larimer	30,721,000	China
Las Animas	4,036,000	China
Lincoln	1,429,000	China
Logan	9,717,000	China
Mesa	16,196,000	China
Mineral	102,000	China
Moffat	1,901,000	China
Montezuma	3,222,000	China
Montrose	3,855,000	China
Morgan	7,976,000	China
Otero	8,136,000	China
Ouray	453,000	China
Park	61,000	China
Phillips	3,072,000	China
Pitkin	1,784,000	China
Prowers	4,526,000	China
Pueblo	40,974,000	China
Rio Blanco	1,642,000	China
Rio Grande	3,710,000	China
Routt	1,762,000	China
Saguache	1,646,000	China

U.S. County	U.S. Church Resources Available for Global Word and Deed Mission (Dollars)	Nation
San Juan	62,000	China
San Miguel	114,000	China
Sedgwick	1,865,000	China
Summit	850,000	China
Teller	1,338,000	China
Washington	1,713,000	China
Weld	28,107,000	China
Yuma	3,144,000	China
Connecticut	$ 1,690,410,000	
Fairfield	192,112,000	Algeria
	8,247,000	Libya
	64,572,000	Morocco
	150,787,000	Sudan
	107,535,000	Tunisia
Hartford	482,980,000	Ethiopa
Litchfield	82,662,000	Sudan
Middlesex	57,799,000	Ethiopa
New Haven	149,938,000	Ethiopa
	241,398,000	Sudan
New London	82,555,000	Ethiopa
Tolland	30,605,000	Ethiopa
Windham	39,220,000	Ethiopa
Delaware	$ 190,091,000	
Kent	16,285,000	India
New Castle	152,316,000	India
Sussex	21,490,000	India
District of Columbia	$ 279,505,000	
District of Columbia	279,505,000	India
Florida	$ 2,521,143,000	
Alachua	27,890,000	India
Baker	1,230,000	India
Bay	23,292,000	India
Bradford	2,558,000	India
Brevard	70,883,000	India
Broward	290,818,000	India
Calhoun	1,601,000	India
Charlotte	12,328,000	India
Citrus	7,570,000	India
Clay	16,522,000	India
Collier	26,784,000	India
Columbia	7,474,000	India
Dade	35,490,000	India
	414,844,000	Sri Lanka
De Soto	3,580,000	India
Dixie	1,217,000	India
Duval	165,659,000	India
Escambia	56,746,000	India
Flagler	2,247,000	India
Franklin	1,420,000	India
Gadsden	4,892,000	India
Gilchrist	1,813,000	India
Glades	918,000	India
Gulf	2,704,000	India
Hamilton	1,795,000	India
Hardee	6,147,000	India
Hendry	6,845,000	India
Hernando	8,176,000	India
Highlands	11,121,000	India
Hillsborough	154,017,000	India
Holmes	3,373,000	India
Indian River	16,201,000	India
Jackson	8,137,000	India
Jefferson	1,551,000	India
Lafayette	947,000	India
Lake	27,294,000	India
Lee	51,458,000	India
Leon	32,488,000	India
Levy	3,625,000	India

U.S. County	U.S. Church Resources Available for Global Word and Deed Mission (Dollars)	Nation	U.S. County	U.S. Church Resources Available for Global Word and Deed Mission (Dollars)	Nation
Liberty	749,000	India	Dade	1,713,000	India
Madison	3,493,000	India	Dawson	1,975,000	India
Manatee	35,035,000	India	Decatur	5,229,000	India
Marion	22,653,000	India	De Kalb	178,015,000	India
Martin	19,446,000	India	Dodge	5,083,000	India
Monroe	14,698,000	India	Dooly	3,453,000	India
Nassau	1,568,000	India	Dougherty	23,652,000	India
	4,407,000	Maldives	Douglas	10,731,000	India
Okaloosa	26,548,000	India	Early	2,849,000	India
Okeechobee	2,959,000	India	Echols	327,000	India
Orange	139,647,000	India	Effingham	4,220,000	India
Osceola	7,978,000	India	Elbert	7,450,000	India
Palm Beach	198,312,000	India	Emanuel	3,662,000	India
Pasco	26,608,000	India	Evans	1,595,000	India
Pinellas	197,122,000	India	Fannin	4,947,000	India
Polk	88,401,000	India	Fayette	9,418,000	India
Putnam	8,861,000	India	Floyd	31,113,000	India
St. Johns	10,030,000	India	Forsyth	10,247,000	India
St. Lucie	14,949,000	India	Franklin	8,048,000	India
Santa Rosa	14,178,000	India	Fulton	236,711,000	India
Sarasota	62,394,000	India	Gilmer	2,176,000	India
Seminole	28,123,000	India	Glascock	998,000	India
Sumter	3,946,000	India	Glynn	17,119,000	India
Suwannee	5,756,000	India	Gordon	8,505,000	India
Taylor	4,135,000	India	Grady	4,860,000	India
Union	727,000	India	Greene	2,262,000	India
Volusia	56,781,000	India	Gwinnett	34,515,000	India
Wakulla	1,320,000	India	Habersham	6,986,000	India
Walton	3,924,000	India	Hall	25,395,000	India
Washington	2,740,000	India	Hancock	1,214,000	India
			Haralson	5,951,000	India
Georgia	$ 1,546,126,000		Harris	2,929,000	India
Appling	4,394,000	India	Hart	6,337,000	India
Atkinson	949,000	India	Heard	1,702,000	India
Bacon	1,944,000	India	Henry	8,627,000	India
Baker	730,000	India	Houston	22,650,000	India
Baldwin	5,806,000	India	Irwin	1,253,000	India
Banks	2,529,000	India	Jackson	6,045,000	India
Barrow	6,284,000	India	Jasper	2,100,000	India
Bartow	11,137,000	India	Jeff Davis	3,691,000	India
Ben Hill	4,686,000	India	Jefferson	4,033,000	India
Berrien	2,732,000	India	Jenkins	1,749,000	India
Bibb	51,760,000	India	Johnson	1,990,000	India
Bleckley	2,846,000	India	Jones	2,108,000	India
Brantley	1,337,000	India	Lamar	3,230,000	India
Brooks	2,748,000	India	Lanier	961,000	India
Bryan	1,668,000	India	Laurens	10,702,000	India
Bulloch	6,228,000	India	Lee	949,000	India
Burke	3,096,000	India	Liberty	3,463,000	India
Butts	3,082,000	India	Lincoln	1,954,000	India
Calhoun	1,217,000	India	Long	836,000	India
Camden	4,292,000	India	Lowndes	16,733,000	India
Candler	1,288,000	India	Lumpkin	1,201,000	India
Carroll	15,232,000	India	McDuffie	4,090,000	India
Catoosa	6,932,000	India	McIntosh	962,000	India
Charlton	1,458,000	India	Macon	3,481,000	India
Chatham	57,276,000	India	Madison	4,078,000	India
Chattahoochee	811,000	India	Marion	751,000	India
Chattooga	6,386,000	India	Meriwether	5,382,000	India
Cherokee	8,381,000	India	Miller	997,000	India
Clarke	16,639,000	India	Mitchell	4,235,000	India
Clay	504,000	India	Monroe	2,989,000	India
Clayton	37,395,000	India	Montgomery	1,436,000	India
Clinch	838,000	India	Morgan	2,644,000	India
Cobb	92,579,000	India	Murray	3,251,000	India
Coffee	4,496,000	India	Muscogee	48,936,000	India
Colquitt	11,524,000	India	Newton	9,844,000	India
Columbia	4,954,000	India	Oconee	2,387,000	India
Cook	2,764,000	India	Oglethorpe	1,363,000	India
Coweta	11,112,000	India	Paulding	5,415,000	India
Crawford	1,158,000	India	Peach	4,448,000	India
Crisp	4,265,000	India	Pickens	1,786,000	India

U.S. County	U.S. Church Resources Available for Global Word and Deed Mission (Dollars)	Nation
Pierce	2,652,000	India
Pike	2,771,000	India
Polk	10,081,000	India
Pulaski	2,536,000	India
Putnam	1,717,000	India
Quitman	234,000	India
Rabun	2,443,000	India
Randolph	1,423,000	India
Richmond	48,542,000	India
Rockdale	7,604,000	India
Schley	667,000	India
Screven	3,806,000	India
Seminole	1,432,000	India
Spalding	16,365,000	India
Stephens	8,130,000	India
Stewart	1,169,000	India
Sumter	6,268,000	India
Talbot	933,000	India
Taliaferro	609,000	India
Tattnall	2,792,000	India
Taylor	1,318,000	India
Telfair	4,109,000	India
Terrell	1,767,000	India
Thomas	11,047,000	India
Tift	8,458,000	India
Toombs	5,463,000	India
Towns	1,581,000	India
Treutlen	785,000	India
Troup	18,129,000	India
Turner	2,528,000	India
Twiggs	1,549,000	India
Union	1,954,000	India
Upson	7,090,000	India
Walker	15,775,000	India
Walton	6,506,000	India
Ware	9,823,000	India
Warren	1,727,000	India
Washington	4,898,000	India
Wayne	5,812,000	India
Webster	503,000	India
Wheeler	1,059,000	India
White	1,843,000	India
Whitfield	19,221,000	India
Wilcox	2,024,000	India
Wilkes	3,076,000	India
Wilkinson	3,007,000	India
Worth	3,306,000	India
Hawaii	**$ 221,845,000**	
Hawaii	244,000	Cook Islands
	5,234,000	Fiji
	1,180,000	Kiribati
	50,000	Niue
	8,488,000	Papua New Guinea
	3,408,000	Samoa, Western
	5,426,000	Solomon Islands
	38,000	Tokelau
	2,209,000	Tonga
	180,000	Tuvalu
	2,664,000	Vanuatu
	148,000	Wallis and Futuna
Honolulu	6,000	Christmas Island
	6,000	Cocos (Keeling) Islands
	128,440,000	Japan
	2,197,000	Pacific Islands (Trust Territory)
	39,093,000	Papua New Guinea
Kalawau	96,000	Papua New Guinea
Kauai	10,272,000	Japan
Maui	12,466,000	Papua New Guinea

U.S. County	U.S. Church Resources Available for Global Word and Deed Mission (Dollars)	Nation
Idaho	**$ 147,056,000**	
Ada	34,110,000	China
Adams	247,000	China
Bannock	6,717,000	China
Bear Lake	105,000	China
Benewah	1,591,000	Mongolia
Bingham	2,874,000	China
Blaine	814,000	China
Boise	226,000	China
Bonner	2,981,000	Mongolia
Bonneville	7,994,000	China
Boundary	1,100,000	Mongolia
Butte	177,000	China
Camas	20,000	China
Canyon	16,711,000	China
Caribou	346,000	China
Cassia	5,427,000	China
Clark	130,000	China
Clearwater	1,438,000	Mongolia
Custer	181,000	China
Elmore	2,710,000	China
Franklin	64,000	China
Fremont	410,000	China
Gem	1,930,000	China
Gooding	1,699,000	China
Idaho	2,993,000	China
Jefferson	117,000	China
Jerome	2,200,000	China
Kootenai	8,705,000	Mongolia
Latah	4,811,000	Mongolia
Lemhi	771,000	China
Lewis	1,685,000	China
Lincoln	529,000	China
Madison	86,000	China
Minidoka	2,603,000	China
Nez Perce	616,000	China
	7,083,000	Mongolia
Oneida	297,000	China
Owyhee	1,455,000	China
Payette	4,070,000	China
Power	944,000	China
Shoshone	3,999,000	Mongolia
Teton	189,000	China
Twin Falls	11,263,000	China
Valley	770,000	China
Washington	1,868,000	China
Illinois	**$ 4,993,696,000**	
Adams	32,346,000	China
Alexander	2,106,000	China
Bond	4,369,000	China
Boone	9,024,000	China
Brown	1,795,000	China
Bureau	15,696,000	China
Calhoun	2,161,000	China
Carroll	5,363,000	China
Cass	5,976,000	China
Champaign	41,910,000	China
Christian	14,868,000	China
Clark	5,582,000	China
Clay	5,282,000	China
Clinton	13,118,000	China
Coles	11,834,000	China
Cook	2,543,903,000	China
Crawford	8,230,000	China
Cumberland	1,758,000	China
De Kalb	27,636,000	China
De Witt	6,065,000	China
Douglas	8,418,000	China
Du Page	356,866,000	China
Edgar	7,363,000	China
Edwards	3,729,000	China

U.S. County	U.S. Church Resources Available for Global Word and Deed Mission (Dollars)	Nation	U.S. County	U.S. Church Resources Available for Global Word and Deed Mission (Dollars)	Nation
Effingham	15,222,000	China	White	7,611,000	China
Fayette	6,848,000	China	Whiteside	29,542,000	China
Ford	8,149,000	China	Will	122,788,000	China
Franklin	17,395,000	China	Williamson	17,451,000	China
Fulton	11,611,000	China	Winnebago	89,130,000	China
Gallatin	1,700,000	China	Woodford	11,575,000	China
Greene	5,333,000	China			
Grundy	14,555,000	China	Indiana	$ 1,663,409,000	
Hamilton	2,825,000	China	Adams	13,547,000	China
Hancock	7,709,000	China	Allen	108,052,000	China
Hardin	704,000	China	Bartholomew	22,534,000	China
Henderson	2,193,000	China	Benton	5,863,000	China
Henry	24,767,000	China	Blackford	3,746,000	China
Iroquois	14,000,000	China	Boone	10,037,000	China
Jackson	16,860,000	China	Brown	1,100,000	China
Jasper	3,231,000	China	Carroll	5,683,000	China
Jefferson	12,603,000	China	Cass	13,181,000	China
Jersey	5,940,000	China	Clark	23,671,000	China
Jo Daviess	7,729,000	China	Clay	7,810,000	China
Johnson	1,910,000	China	Clinton	9,734,000	China
Kane	126,957,000	China	Crawford	2,156,000	China
Kankakee	40,803,000	China	Daviess	9,353,000	China
Kendall	14,169,000	China	Dearborn	10,134,000	China
Knox	19,805,000	China	Decatur	10,363,000	China
Lake	191,578,000	China	De Kalb	10,753,000	China
La Salle	52,743,000	China	Delaware	24,397,000	China
Lawrence	5,637,000	China	Dubois	19,147,000	China
Lee	14,691,000	China	Elkhart	43,260,000	China
Livingston	15,613,000	China	Fayette	6,832,000	China
Logan	13,784,000	China	Floyd	22,829,000	China
McDonough	10,776,000	China	Fountain	4,369,000	China
McHenry	63,794,000	China	Franklin	5,020,000	China
McLean	41,920,000	China	Fulton	4,540,000	China
Macon	46,369,000	China	Gibson	9,992,000	China
Macoupin	18,399,000	China	Grant	17,362,000	China
Madison	103,205,000	China	Greene	6,875,000	China
Marion	17,400,000	China	Hamilton	27,058,000	China
Marshall	5,471,000	China	Hancock	12,834,000	China
Mason	7,144,000	China	Harrison	6,878,000	China
Massac	5,524,000	China	Hendricks	18,155,000	China
Menard	4,687,000	China	Henry	12,829,000	China
Mercer	5,028,000	China	Howard	28,334,000	China
Monroe	11,112,000	China	Huntington	13,516,000	China
Montgomery	14,015,000	China	Jackson	14,553,000	China
Morgan	14,954,000	China	Jasper	7,460,000	China
Moultrie	4,619,000	China	Jay	6,553,000	China
Ogle	14,223,000	China	Jefferson	7,748,000	China
Peoria	79,319,000	China	Jennings	4,712,000	China
Perry	11,022,000	China	Johnson	19,595,000	China
Piatt	6,493,000	China	Knox	14,825,000	China
Pike	4,776,000	China	Kosciusko	11,746,000	China
Pope	752,000	China	Lagrange	6,570,000	China
Pulaski	1,887,000	China	Lake	190,000,000	China
Putnam	1,814,000	China	La Porte	37,293,000	China
Randolph	13,686,000	China	Lawrence	12,729,000	China
Richland	6,164,000	China	Madison	38,591,000	China
Rock Island	69,294,000	China	Marion	245,039,000	China
St. Clair	77,067,000	China	Marshall	10,850,000	China
Saline	11,927,000	China	Martin	3,160,000	China
Sangamon	77,500,000	China	Miami	9,557,000	China
Schuyler	1,903,000	China	Monroe	16,488,000	China
Scott	2,853,000	China	Montgomery	11,102,000	China
Shelby	8,060,000	China	Morgan	12,240,000	China
Stark	2,582,000	China	Newton	3,826,000	China
Stephenson	19,002,000	China	Noble	7,700,000	China
Tazewell	53,872,000	China	Ohio	1,003,000	China
Union	7,527,000	China	Orange	4,042,000	China
Vermillion	30,032,000	China	Owen	2,683,000	China
Wabash	5,764,000	China	Parke	3,448,000	China
Warren	8,056,000	China	Perry	5,398,000	China
Washington	7,395,000	China	Pike	3,660,000	China
Wayne	5,750,000	China	Porter	32,425,000	China

U.S. County	U.S. Church Resources Available for Global Word and Deed Mission (Dollars)	Nation
Posey	8,478,000	China
Pulaski	4,720,000	China
Putnam	6,034,000	China
Randolph	6,871,000	China
Ripley	9,454,000	China
Rush	7,233,000	China
St. Joseph	79,469,000	China
Scott	4,431,000	China
Shelby	11,780,000	China
Spencer	7,143,000	China
Starke	3,401,000	China
Steuben	4,867,000	China
Sullivan	5,872,000	China
Switzerland	1,302,000	China
Tippecanoe	32,004,000	China
Tipton	4,707,000	China
Union	1,443,000	China
Vanderburgh	73,637,000	China
Vermillion	3,496,000	China
Vigo	22,159,000	China
Wabash	10,631,000	China
Warren	1,915,000	China
Warrick	10,219,000	China
Washington	4,265,000	China
Wayne	18,800,000	China
Wells	7,597,000	China
White	7,923,000	China
Whitley	6,618,000	China
Iowa	$ 1,251,826,000	
Adair	3,525,000	China
Adams	1,756,000	China
Allamakee	6,970,000	China
Appanoose	3,722,000	China
Audubon	4,278,000	China
Benton	9,350,000	China
Black Hawk	61,536,000	China
Boone	11,371,000	China
Bremer	13,274,000	China
Buchanan	9,711,000	China
Buena Vista	12,243,000	China
Butler	7,825,000	China
Calhoun	9,943,000	China
Carroll	15,934,000	China
Cass	8,483,000	China
Cedar	6,620,000	China
Cerro Gordo	25,340,000	China
Cherokee	8,475,000	China
Chickasaw	7,849,000	China
Clarke	2,254,000	China
Clay	9,720,000	China
Clayton	8,831,000	China
Clinton	24,672,000	China
Crawford	9,789,000	China
Dallas	9,943,000	China
Davis	2,082,000	China
Decatur	1,507,000	China
Delaware	7,325,000	China
Des Moines	18,268,000	China
Dickinson	6,596,000	China
Dubuque	53,281,000	China
Emmet	8,361,000	China
Fayette	11,807,000	China
Floyd	7,728,000	China
Franklin	6,188,000	China
Fremont	2,715,000	China
Greene	7,472,000	China
Grundy	7,439,000	China
Guthrie	4,442,000	China
Hamilton	10,126,000	China
Hancock	7,216,000	China
Hardin	11,559,000	China

U.S. County	U.S. Church Resources Available for Global Word and Deed Mission (Dollars)	Nation
Harrison	5,762,000	China
Henry	6,369,000	China
Howard	5,940,000	China
Humboldt	7,313,000	China
Ida	4,725,000	China
Iowa	7,251,000	China
Jackson	8,936,000	China
Jasper	14,601,000	China
Jefferson	5,095,000	China
Johnson	18,875,000	China
Jones	7,028,000	China
Keokuk	5,495,000	China
Kossuth	13,707,000	China
Lee	17,870,000	China
Linn	75,092,000	China
Louisa	2,496,000	China
Lucas	2,846,000	China
Lyon	6,683,000	China
Madison	3,815,000	China
Mahaska	8,448,000	China
Marion	12,908,000	China
Marshall	18,797,000	China
Mills	3,990,000	China
Mitchell	6,893,000	China
Monona	4,911,000	China
Monroe	3,037,000	China
Montgomery	5,908,000	China
Muscatine	16,806,000	China
O'Brien	11,342,000	China
Osceola	4,820,000	China
Page	8,313,000	China
Palo Alto	7,952,000	China
Plymouth	12,142,000	China
Pocahontas	8,063,000	China
Polk	119,070,000	China
Potawattamie	26,098,000	China
Poweshiek	7,064,000	China
Ringgold	1,928,000	China
Sac	9,366,000	China
Scott	61,248,000	China
Shelby	8,179,000	China
Sioux	15,740,000	China
Story	24,366,000	China
Tama	7,901,000	China
Taylor	2,802,000	China
Union	4,701,000	China
Van Buren	2,182,000	China
Wapello	13,076,000	China
Warren	9,386,000	China
Washington	8,889,000	China
Wayne	2,459,000	China
Webster	25,040,000	China
Winnebago	8,002,000	China
Winneshiek	8,918,000	China
Woodbury	48,861,000	China
Worth	5,009,000	China
Wright	9,786,000	China
Kansas	$ 949,925,000	
Allen	5,332,000	China
Anderson	3,431,000	China
Atchison	6,067,000	China
Barber	3,679,000	China
Barton	19,813,000	China
Bourbon	5,038,000	China
Brown	4,789,000	China
Butler	16,248,000	China
Chase	1,405,000	China
Chautauqua	1,352,000	China
Cherokee	5,852,000	China
Cheyenne	1,632,000	China
Clark	2,459,000	China

U.S. County	U.S. Church Resources Available for Global Word and Deed Mission (Dollars)	Nation	U.S. County	U.S. Church Resources Available for Global Word and Deed Mission (Dollars)	Nation
Clay	3,708,000	China	Scott	4,636,000	China
Cloud	5,826,000	China	Sedgwick	153,228,000	China
Coffey	3,363,000	China	Seward	8,429,000	China
Comanche	2,390,000	China	Shawnee	58,710,000	China
Cowley	12,862,000	China	Sheridan	2,083,000	China
Crawford	11,371,000	China	Sherman	2,382,000	China
Decatur	2,480,000	China	Smith	2,731,000	China
Dickinson	8,313,000	China	Stafford	3,755,000	China
Doniphan	2,905,000	China	Stanton	791,000	China
Douglas	12,434,000	China	Stevens	3,321,000	China
Edwards	2,441,000	China	Sumner	11,480,000	China
Elk	1,317,000	China	Thomas	3,252,000	China
Ellis	12,409,000	China	Trego	2,179,000	China
Ellsworth	3,487,000	China	Wabaunsee	2,213,000	China
Finney	13,856,000	China	Wallace	914,000	China
Ford	13,595,000	China	Washington	3,712,000	China
Franklin	6,924,000	China	Wichita	7,712,000	China
Geary	7,038,000	China	Wilson	3,052,000	China
Gove	2,002,000	China	Woodson	1,518,000	China
Graham	1,877,000	China	Wyandotte	50,111,000	China
Grant	3,234,000	China			
Gray	2,667,000	China	Kentucky	$ 1,182,503,000	
Greeley	1,816,000	China	Adair	3,615,000	China
Greenwood	2,881,000	China	Allen	3,097,000	China
Hamilton	1,328,000	China	Anderson	5,152,000	China
Harper	4,029,000	China	Ballard	3,710,000	China
Harvey	13,966,000	China	Barren	9,352,000	China
Haskell	2,768,000	China	Bath	2,281,000	China
Hodgeman	1,421,000	China	Bell	8,826,000	China
Jackson	3,004,000	China	Boone	16,608,000	China
Jefferson	4,629,000	China	Bourbon	8,848,000	China
Jewell	2,012,000	China	Boyd	22,884,000	China
Johnson	140,727,000	China	Boyle	11,115,000	China
Kearny	1,585,000	China	Bracken	2,796,000	China
Kingman	4,584,000	China	Breathitt	1,431,000	China
Kiowa	2,430,000	China	Breckinridge	5,189,000	China
Labette	7,965,000	China	Bullitt	9,520,000	China
Lane	2,277,000	China	Butler	3,253,000	China
Leavenworth	12,646,000	China	Caldwell	7,528,000	China
Lincoln	1,973,000	China	Calloway	9,861,000	China
Linn	2,158,000	China	Campbell	31,984,000	China
Logan	1,872,000	China	Carlisle	2,490,000	China
Lyon	10,524,000	China	Carroll	3,339,000	China
McPherson	14,355,000	China	Carter	1,820,000	China
Marion	6,350,000	China	Casey	2,784,000	China
Marshall	5,931,000	China	Christian	15,020,000	China
Meade	3,538,000	China	Clark	9,629,000	China
Miami	6,326,000	China	Clay	3,307,000	China
Mitchell	5,364,000	China	Clinton	1,505,000	China
Montgomery	16,981,000	China	Crittenden	2,973,000	China
Morris	2,144,000	China	Cumberland	1,517,000	China
Morton	2,944,000	China	Daviess	43,005,000	China
Nemaha	4,384,000	China	Edmonson	1,274,000	China
Neosho	6,902,000	China	Elliott	113,000	China
Ness	2,981,000	China	Estill	3,015,000	China
Norton	2,377,000	China	Fayette	74,779,000	China
Osage	2,934,000	China	Fleming	2,468,000	China
Osborne	3,130,000	China	Floyd	3,442,000	China
Ottawa	1,978,000	China	Franklin	19,936,000	China
Pawnee	3,580,000	China	Fulton	4,422,000	China
Phillips	3,214,000	China	Gallatin	1,750,000	China
Pottawatomie	4,605,000	China	Garrard	3,422,000	China
Pratt	5,187,000	China	Grant	4,409,000	China
Rawlins	1,558,000	China	Graves	15,114,000	China
Reno	24,687,000	China	Grayson	3,952,000	China
Republic	2,541,000	China	Green	4,265,000	China
Rice	5,994,000	China	Greenup	7,018,000	China
Riley	9,746,000	China	Hancock	3,673,000	China
Rooks	3,691,000	China	Hardin	18,560,000	China
Rush	3,199,000	China	Harlan	10,311,000	China
Russell	5,818,000	China	Harrison	5,766,000	China
Saline	21,086,000	China	Hart	4,319,000	China

U.S. County	U.S. Church Resources Available for Global Word and Deed Mission (Dollars)	Nation	U.S. County	U.S. Church Resources Available for Global Word and Deed Mission (Dollars)	Nation
Henderson	17,312,000	China	Louisiana	$ 1,546,763,000	
Henry	4,850,000	China	Acadia	29,802,000	Bangladesh
Hickman	2,256,000	China	Allen	4,903,000	Bangladesh
Hopkins	17,626,000	China	Ascension	17,541,000	Bangladesh
Jackson	1,420,000	China	Assumption	7,173,000	Bangladesh
Jefferson	308,271,000	China	Avoyelles	10,862,000	Bangladesh
Jessamine	4,658,000	China	Beauregard	7,706,000	Bangladesh
Johnson	2,294,000	China	Bienville	4,375,000	Bangladesh
Kenton	50,569,000	China	Bossier	20,485,000	Bangladesh
Knott	880,000	China	Caddo	99,388,000	Bangladesh
Knox	6,296,000	China	Calcasieu	73,412,000	Bangladesh
Larue	4,164,000	China	Caldwell	1,946,000	Bangladesh
Laurel	7,145,000	China	Cameron	3,125,000	Bangladesh
Lawrence	988,000	China	Catahoula	2,161,000	Bangladesh
Lee	1,463,000	China	Claiborne	5,979,000	Bangladesh
Leslie	950,000	China	Concordia	5,121,000	Bangladesh
Letcher	2,232,000	China	De Soto	5,405,000	Bangladesh
Lewis	1,533,000	China	East Baton Rouge	142,292,000	Bangladesn
Lincoln	5,541,000	China	East Carroll	2,025,000	Bangladesh
Livingston	3,551,000	China	East Feliciana	2,916,000	Bangladesh
Logan	9,669,000	China	Evangeline	10,521,000	Bangladesh
Lyon	2,063,000	China	Franklin	5,105,000	Bangladesh
McCracken	27,907,000	China	Grant	3,874,000	Bangladesh
McCreary	1,275,000	China	Iberia	32,658,000	Bangladesh
McLean	3,494,000	China	Iberville	8,071,000	Bangladesh
Madison	11,387,000	China	Jackson	5,106,000	Bangladesh
Magoffin	395,000	China	Jefferson	201,668,000	Bangladesh
Marion	6,291,000	China	Jefferson Davis	10,815,000	Bangladesh
Marshall	8,623,000	China	Lafayette	83,119,000	Bangladesh
Martin	892,000	China	Lafourche	39,280,000	Bangladesh
Mason	7,026,000	China	La Salle	4,661,000	Bangladesh
Meade	4,151,000	China	Lincoln	9,874,000	Bangladesh
Menifee	237,000	China	Livingston	22,929,000	Bangladesh
Mercer	8,241,000	China	Madison	2,111,000	Bangladesh
Metcalfe	1,441,000	China	Morehouse	9,498,000	Bangladesh
Monroe	2,306,000	China	Natchitoches	8,672,000	Bangladesh
Montgomery	5,092,000	China	Orleans	194,162,000	Bangladesh
Morgan	819,000	China	Ouachita	43,243,000	Bangladesh
Muhlenberg	14,579,000	China	Palquemines	11,743,000	Bangladesh
Nelson	10,541,000	China	Pointe Coupee	7,802,000	Bangladesh
Nicholas	1,922,000	China	Rapides	38,648,000	Bangladesh
Ohio	8,256,000	China	Red River	2,387,000	Bangladesh
Oldham	6,712,000	China	Richland	6,641,000	Bangladesh
Owen	3,513,000	China	Sabine	5,097,000	Bangladesh
Owsley	413,000	China	St. Bernard	45,669,000	Bangladesh
Pendleton	4,234,000	China	St. Charles	17,730,000	Bangladesh
Perry	5,009,000	China	St. Helena	2,007,000	Bangladesh
Pike	8,109,000	China	St. James	9,856,000	Bangladesh
Powell	1,691,000	China	St. John The Baptist	11,103,000	Bangladesh
Pulaski	13,229,000	China	St. Landry	31,070,000	Bangladesh
Robertson	419,000	China	St. Martin	11,935,000	Bangladesh
Rockcastle	2,722,000	China	St. Mary	28,258,000	Bangladesh
Rowan	1,828,000	China	St. Tammany	35,308,000	Bangladesh
Russell	2,614,000	China	Tangipahoa	17,534,000	Bangladesh
Scott	6,849,000	China	Tensas	1,302,000	Bangladesh
Shelby	9,362,000	China	Terrebonne	46,558,000	Bangladesh
Simpson	4,979,000	China	Union	6,173,000	Bangladesh
Spencer	2,689,000	China	Vermilion	18,341,000	Bangladesh
Taylor	7,933,000	China	Vernon	8,363,000	Bangladesh
Todd	4,155,000	China	Washington	11,571,000	Bangladesh
Trigg	4,024,000	China	Webster	15,668,000	Bangladesh
Trimble	1,514,000	China	West Baton Rouge	4,086,000	Bangladesh
Union	7,890,000	China	West Carroll	3,298,000	Bangladesh
Warren	20,280,000	China	West Feliciana	1,804,000	Bangladesh
Washington	5,200,000	China	Winn	4,827,000	Bangladesh
Wayne	3,632,000	China			
Webster	6,010,000	China	Maine	$ 272,269,000	
Whitley	11,192,000	China	Androscoggin	13,444,000	Botswana
Wolfe	451,000	China		15,919,000	South Africa
Woodford	8,797,000	China	Aroostook	25,406,000	South Africa
				708,000	Swaziland

U.S. County	U.S. Church Resources Available for Global Word and Deed Mission (Dollars)	Nation	U.S. County	U.S. Church Resources Available for Global Word and Deed Mission (Dollars)	Nation
Cumberland	55,617,000	Angola	Suffolk	331,911,000	Tanzania
	10,079,000	Namibia	Worchester	286,104,000	Zaire
Franklin	5,099,000	South Africa			
Hancock	6,446,000	Lesotho	Michigan	$ 2,976,250,000	
Kennebec	30,371,000	South Africa	Alcona	1,259,000	China
Knox	6,159,000	South Africa	Alger	2,257,000	China
Lincoln	4,287,000	South Africa	Allegan	16,041,000	China
Oxford	8,327,000	Angola	Alpena	14,993,000	China
Penobscot	19,280,000	Lesotho	Antrim	2,904,000	China
	11,118,000	Swaziland	Arenac	3,913,000	China
Piscataquis	3,358,000	South Africa	Baraga	3,344,000	China
Sagadahoc	1,326,000	Botswana	Barry	5,769,000	China
	3,272,000	Namibia	Bay	54,989,000	China
Somerset	8,525,000	South Africa	Benzie	1,783,000	China
Waldo	2,209,000	Lesotho	Berrien	50,445,000	China
Washington	4,663,000	Lesotho	Branch	7,246,000	China
York	36,656,000	Angola	Calhoun	36,034,000	China
			Cass	6,672,000	China
Maryland	$ 1,326,901,000		Charlevoix	5,091,000	China
Allegany	29,098,000	India	Cheboygan	4,598,000	China
Anne Arundel	100,680,000	India	Chippewa	6,062,000	China
Baltimore	218,797,000	India	Clare	3,106,000	China
Baltimore City	204,918,000	India	Clinton	14,774,000	China
Calvert	6,247,000	India	Crawford	1,466,000	China
Caroline	5,238,000	India	Delta	15,419,000	China
Carroll	30,569,000	India	Dickinson	12,493,000	China
Cecil	11,132,000	India	Eaton	13,606,000	China
Charles	19,136,000	India	Emmet	7,445,000	China
Dorchester	7,784,000	India	Genesee	121,049,000	China
Frederick	36,910,000	India	Gladwin	3,273,000	China
Garrett	5,871,000	India	Gogebic	7,506,000	China
Harford	40,191,000	India	Grand Traverse	16,986,000	China
Howard	39,127,000	India	Gratiot	10,993,000	China
Kent	5,050,000	India	Hillsdale	5,993,000	China
Montgomery	285,981,000	India	Houghton	9,290,000	China
Prince Georges	186,792,000	India	Huron	17,944,000	China
Queen Annes	8,499,000	India	Ingham	78,992,000	China
St. Marys	11,733,000	India	Ionia	10,281,000	China
Somerset	4,174,000	India	Iosco	6,030,000	China
Talbot	10,255,000	India	Iron	5,155,000	China
Washington	34,609,000	India	Isabella	10,047,000	China
Wicomico	15,522,000	India	Jackson	34,046,000	China
Worcester	8,588,000	India	Kalamazoo	56,264,000	China
			Kalkaska	1,408,000	China
Massachusetts	$ 2,832,680,000		Kent	162,473,000	China
Barnstable	16,045,000	Kenya	Keweenaw	364,000	China
	35,612,000	Uganda	Lake	635,000	China
Berkshire	45,806,000	Central African Republic	Lapeer	10,833,000	China
	17,421,000	Zaire	Leelanau	5,045,000	China
Bristol	47,407,000	Rwanda	Lenawee	24,500,000	China
	157,336,000	Uganda	Livingston	21,911,000	China
Dukes	2,685,000	Kenya	Luce	1,310,000	China
Essex	9,885,000	Comoros	Mackinac	2,715,000	China
	217,192,000	Madagascar	Macomb	313,574,000	China
	17,098,000	Mauritius	Manistee	8,831,000	China
	1,359,000	Mayotte	Marquette	21,668,000	China
	34,195,000	Mozambique	Mason	6,382,000	China
	609,000	Seychelles	Mecosta	4,352,000	China
	1,982,000	Tanzania	Menominee	9,954,000	China
Franklin	17,577,000	Zaire	Midland	28,227,000	China
Hampden	205,097,000	Zaire	Missaukee	2,041,000	China
Hampshire	23,891,000	Zaire	Monroe	45,608,000	China
Middlesex	155,651,000	Malawi	Montcalm	10,069,000	China
	242,953,000	Mozambique	Montmorency	1,955,000	China
	189,871,000	Zaire	Muskegon	39,501,000	China
	129,521,000	Zambia	Newaygo	5,826,000	China
	161,583,000	Zimbabwe	Oakland	363,464,000	China
Nantucket	3,172,000	Kenya	Oceana	4,520,000	China
Norfolk	108,419,000	Burundi	Ogemaw	2,651,000	China
	87,502,000	Rwanda	Ontonagon	2,713,000	China
	140,591,000	Tanzania	Osceola	3,188,000	China
Plymouth	144,205,000	Uganda	Oscoda	064,000	China

U.S. County	U.S. Church Resources Available for Global Word and Deed Mission (Dollars)	Nation	U.S. County	U.S. Church Resources Available for Global Word and Deed Mission (Dollars)	Nation
Otsego	5,472,000	China	Otter Tail	20,473,000	China
Ottawa	68,656,000	China	Pennington	7,559,000	China
Presque Isle	4,787,000	China	Pine	5,180,000	China
Roscommon	2,023,000	China	Pipestone	6,967,000	China
Saginaw	90,149,000	China	Polk	17,135,000	China
St. Clair	41,511,000	China	Pope	5,296,000	China
St. Joseph	14,705,000	China	Ramsey	239,545,000	China
Sanilac	8,950,000	China	Red Lake	3,001,000	China
Schoolcraft	3,970,000	China	Redwood	12,477,000	China
Shiawassee	19,364,000	China	Renville	12,942,000	China
Tuscola	15,870,000	China	Rice	18,943,000	China
Van Buren	11,710,000	China	Rock	6,786,000	China
Washtenaw	71,970,000	China	Roseau	5,954,000	China
Wayne	819,507,000	China	St. Louis	88,881,000	China
Wexford	5,666,000	China	Scott	24,243,000	China
			Sherburne	9,231,000	China
Minnesota	$ 1,925,115,000		Sibley	8,595,000	China
Aitkin	3,051,000	China	Stearns	45,117,000	China
Anoka	81,975,000	China	Steele	19,093,000	China
Becker	9,164,000	China	Stevens	5,379,000	China
Beltrami	6,547,000	China	Swift	5,810,000	China
Benton	11,106,000	China	Todd	7,918,000	China
Big Stone	4,367,000	China	Traverse	2,933,000	China
Blue Earth	24,725,000	China	Wabasha	10,141,000	China
Brown	17,783,000	China	Wadena	4,892,000	China
Carlton	9,730,000	China	Waseca	10,103,000	China
Carver	16,588,000	China	Washington	47,828,000	China
Cass	4,157,000	China	Watonwan	7,657,000	China
Chippewa	7,725,000	China	Wilkin	3,874,000	China
Chisago	8,371,000	China	Winona	20,964,000	China
Clay	19,812,000	China	Wright	19,844,000	China
Clearwater	1,747,000	China	Yellow Medicine	7,276,000	China
Cook	1,269,000	China			
Cottonwood	9,340,000	China	Mississippi	$ 691,406,000	
Crow Wing	13,171,000	China	Adams	10,924,000	India
Dakota	89,648,000	China	Alcorn	10,872,000	India
Dodge	6,073,000	China	Amite	4,362,000	India
Douglas	11,167,000	China	Attala	4,874,000	India
Faribault	12,116,000	China	Benton	1,071,000	India
Fillmore	12,236,000	China	Bolivar	6,943,000	India
Freeborn	21,636,000	China	Calhoun	5,305,000	India
Goodhue	22,564,000	China	Carroll	2,227,000	India
Grant	3,588,000	China	Chickasaw	4,901,000	India
Hennepin	486,409,000	China	Choctaw	2,664,000	India
Houston	8,434,000	China	Claiborne	1,896,000	India
Hubbard	2,995,000	China	Clarke	5,515,000	India
Isanti	6,616,000	China	Clay	5,192,000	India
Itasca	11,140,000	China	Coahoma	5,770,000	India
Jackson	7,589,000	China	Copiah	6,827,000	India
Kanabec	3,822,000	China	Covington	3,906,000	India
Kandiyohi	16,777,000	China	De Soto	14,950,000	India
Kittson	3,699,000	China	Forrest	22,846,000	India
Koochiching	5,593,000	China	Franklin	2,309,000	India
Lac Qui Parle	6,616,000	China	George	4,183,000	India
Lake	4,558,000	China	Greene	1,909,000	India
Lake of the Woods	1,264,000	China	Grenada	4,452,000	India
Le Sueur	11,800,000	China	Hancock	5,597,000	Bangladesh
Lincoln	4,061,000	China	Harrison	45,569,000	Bangladesh
Lyon	12,973,000	China	Hinds	96,510,000	India
McLeod	19,849,000	China	Holmes	3,249,000	India
Mahnomen	3,009,000	China	Humphreys	1,932,000	India
Marshall	8,380,000	China	Issaquena	133,000	India
Martin	17,200,000	China	Itawamba	5,024,000	India
Meeker	10,085,000	China	Jackson	29,589,000	India
Mille Lacs	7,745,000	China	Jasper	4,707,000	India
Morrison	10,907,000	China	Jefferson	1,205,000	India
Mower	23,811,000	China	Jefferson Davis	3,039,000	India
Murray	7,196,000	China	Jones	22,850,000	India
Nicollet	10,937,000	China	Kemper	1,883,000	India
Nobles	14,793,000	China	Lafayette	6,999,000	India
Norman	6,601,000	China	Lamar	4,314,000	India
Olmsted	48,563,000	China	Lauderdale	27,490,000	India

U.S. County	U.S. Church Resources Available for Global Word and Deed Mission (Dollars)	Nation	U.S. County	U.S. Church Resources Available for Global Word and Deed Mission (Dollars)	Nation
Lawrence	2,971,000	India	Cole	27,688,000	China
Leake	4,312,000	India	Cooper	6,367,000	China
Lee	22,969,000	India	Crawford	4,220,000	China
Leflore	8,472,000	India	Dade	2,706,000	China
Lincoln	10,119,000	India	Dallas	1,887,000	China
Lowndes	13,940,000	India	Daviess	2,884,000	China
Madison	6,667,000	India	De Kalb	2,298,000	China
Marion	6,993,000	India	Dent	3,707,000	China
Marshall	4,948,000	India	Douglas	908,000	China
Monroe	9,200,000	India	Dunklin	9,425,000	China
Montgomery	3,365,000	India	Franklin	28,935,000	China
Neshoba	6,849,000	India	Gasconade	4,802,000	China
Newton	5,678,000	India	Gentry	3,646,000	China
Noxubee	2,343,000	India	Greene	61,768,000	China
Oktibbeha	8,475,000	India	Grundy	4,952,000	China
Panola	7,868,000	India	Harrison	3,816,000	China
Pearl River	449,000	Bangladesh	Henry	9,140,000	China
	9,671,000	India	Hickory	933,000	China
Perry	2,690,000	India	Holt	2,694,000	China
Pike	9,543,000	India	Howard	3,745,000	China
Pontotoc	6,401,000	India	Howell	6,948,000	China
Prentiss	4,969,000	India	Iron	2,828,000	China
Quitman	2,540,000	India	Jackson	215,719,000	China
Rankin	18,355,000	India	Jasper	30,400,000	China
Scott	6,110,000	India	Jefferson	36,857,000	China
Sharkey	1,258,000	India	Johnson	7,571,000	China
Simpson	7,996,000	India	Knox	2,030,000	China
Smith	4,603,000	India	Laclede	6,153,000	China
Stone	2,647,000	India	Lafayette	12,778,000	China
Sunflower	5,668,000	India	Lawrence	8,515,000	China
Tallahatchie	2,699,000	India	Lewis	3,881,000	China
Tate	5,126,000	India	Lincoln	7,372,000	China
Tippah	5,718,000	India	Linn	6,589,000	China
Tishomingo	4,820,000	India	Livingston	8,433,000	China
Tunica	1,241,000	India	McDonald	2,253,000	China
Union	9,241,000	India	Macon	5,894,000	China
Walthall	2,658,000	India	Madison	2,241,000	China
Warren	16,078,000	India	Maries	1,787,000	China
Washington	15,396,000	India	Marion	11,969,000	China
Wayne	3,765,000	India	Mercer	1,515,000	China
Webster	3,598,000	India	Miller	6,480,000	China
Wilkinson	2,088,000	India	Mississippi	4,272,000	China
Winston	5,618,000	India	Moniteau	5,596,000	China
Yalobusha	4,270,000	India	Monroe	4,034,000	China
Yazoo	7,033,000	India	Montgomery	4,293,000	China
			Morgan	3,208,000	China
Missouri	$ 1,761,174,000		New Madrid	4,974,000	China
Adair	4,884,000	China	Newton	8,950,000	China
Andrew	3,261,000	China	Nodaway	7,143,000	China
Atchison	3,908,000	China	Oregon	1,492,000	China
Audrain	12,203,000	China	Osage	4,642,000	China
Barry	8,333,000	China	Ozark	1,260,000	China
Barton	3,453,000	China	Pemiscot	5,925,000	China
Bates	5,657,000	China	Perry	8,267,000	China
Benton	3,457,000	China	Pettis	14,246,000	China
Bollinger	1,342,000	China	Phelps	8,723,000	China
Boone	25,680,000	China	Pike	6,259,000	China
Buchanan	30,785,000	China	Platte	14,905,000	China
Butler	7,050,000	China	Polk	4,134,000	China
Caldwell	3,066,000	China	Pulaski	5,969,000	China
Callaway	8,185,000	China	Putnam	1,197,000	China
Camden	4,327,000	China	Ralls	2,205,000	China
Cape Girardeau	23,306,000	China	Randolph	8,279,000	China
Carroll	6,226,000	China	Ray	7,457,000	China
Carter	636,000	China	Reynolds	1,406,000	China
Cass	14,882,000	China	Ripley	1,680,000	China
Cedar	2,039,000	China	St. Charles	45,347,000	China
Chariton	4,968,000	China	St. Clair	1,898,000	China
Christian	5,658,000	China	St. Francois	13,450,000	China
Clark	2,715,000	China	St. Louis	501,588,000	China
Clay	51,717,000	China	St. Louis City	159,824,000	China
Clinton	4,473,000	China	Ste. Genevieve	6,584,000	China

U.S. County	U.S. Church Resources Available for Global Word and Deed Mission (Dollars)	Nation	U.S. County	U.S. Church Resources Available for Global Word and Deed Mission (Dollars)	Nation
			Valley	2,991,000	China
Saline	11,244,000	China	Wheatland	656,000	China
Schuyler	1,200,000	China	Wibaux	390,000	China
Scotland	2,117,000	China	Yellowstone	38,592,000	China
Scott	11,882,000	China	Yellowstone National	68,000	China
Shannon	1,098,000	China	Park		
Shelby	3,632,000	China			
Stoddard	5,338,000	China	Nebraska	$ 679,646,000	
Stone	2,378,000	China	Adams	15,115,000	China
Sullivan	2,246,000	China	Antelope	3,325,000	China
Taney	4,466,000	China	Arthur	148,000	China
Texas	4,621,000	China	Banner	109,000	China
Vernon	5,025,000	China	Blaine	178,000	China
Warren	4,666,000	China	Boone	3,450,000	China
Washington	3,067,000	China	Box Butte	4,593,000	China
Wayne	1,426,000	China	Boyd	1,407,000	China
Webster	5,595,000	China	Brown	1,257,000	China
Worth	1,045,000	China	Buffalo	12,729,000	China
Wright	3,976,000	China	Burt	4,283,000	China
			Butler	3,678,000	China
Montana	$ 216,768,000		Cass	6,207,000	China
Beaverhead	1,759,000	China	Cedar	5,581,000	China
Big Horn	2,386,000	China	Chase	1,854,000	China
Blaine	1,868,000	China	Cherry	2,485,000	China
Broadwater	487,000	China	Cheyenne	6,391,000	China
Carbon	1,538,000	China	Clay	3,368,000	China
Carter	236,000	China	Colfax	4,793,000	China
Cascade	22,438,000	China	Cuming	6,221,000	China
Chouteau	3,360,000	China	Custer	4,659,000	China
Custer	5,562,000	China	Dakota	5,286,000	China
Daniels	1,642,000	China	Dawes	2,433,000	China
Dawson	5,489,000	China	Dawson	10,797,000	China
Deer Lodge	2,092,000	China	Deuel	1,851,000	China
Fallon	1,535,000	China	Dixon	3,114,000	China
Fergus	3,690,000	China	Dodge	23,105,000	China
Flathead	12,235,000	China	Douglas	190,835,000	China
Gallatin	8,986,000	China	Dundy	1,330,000	China
Garfield	360,000	China	Fillmore	3,671,000	China
Glacier	4,862,000	China	Franklin	2,167,000	China
Golden Valley	274,000	China	Frontier	1,208,000	China
Granite	388,000	China	Furnas	3,251,000	China
Hill	5,258,000	China	Gage	13,076,000	China
Jefferson	1,081,000	China	Garden	982,000	China
Judith Basin	407,000	China	Garfield	829,000	China
Lake	3,108,000	China	Gosper	703,000	China
Lewis and Clark	13,672,000	China	Grant	431,000	China
Liberty	1,282,000	China	Greeley	1,795,000	China
Lincoln	2,782,000	China	Hall	24,953,000	China
McCone	918,000	China	Hamilton	3,172,000	China
Madison	530,000	China	Harlan	1,718,000	China
Meagher	360,000	China	Hayes	206,000	China
Mineral	231,000	China	Hitchcock	1,633,000	China
Missoula	13,888,000	China	Holt	4,823,000	China
Musselshell	970,000	China	Hooker	378,000	China
Park	2,353,000	China	Howard	2,169,000	China
Petroleum	119,000	China	Jefferson	4,914,000	China
Phillips	1,592,000	China	Johnson	2,262,000	China
Pondera	2,225,000	China	Kearney	3,124,000	China
Powder River	548,000	China	Keith	4,793,000	China
Powell	1,530,000	China	Keya Paha	266,000	China
Prairie	559,000	China	Kimball	2,778,000	China
Ravalli	2,835,000	China	Knox	4,302,000	China
Richland	5,182,000	China	Lancaster	73,467,000	China
Roosevelt	3,736,000	China	Lincoln	13,525,000	China
Rosebud	2,566,000	China	Logan	278,000	China
Sanders	1,197,000	China	Loup	53,000	China
Sheridan	3,033,000	China	McPherson	100,000	China
Silver Bow	13,888,000	China	Madison	19,186,000	China
Stillwater	939,000	China	Merrick	3,272,000	China
Sweet Grass	983,000	China	Morrill	2,045,000	China
Teton	2,101,000	China	Nance	1,803,000	China
Toole	2,779,000	China	Nemaha	3,267,000	China
Treasure	232,000	China			

U.S. County	U.S. Church Resources Available for Global Word and Deed Mission (Dollars)	Nation
Nuckolls	2,884,000	China
Otoe	7,395,000	China
Pawnee	1,597,000	China
Perkins	2,402,000	China
Phelps	5,481,000	China
Pierce	3,882,000	China
Platte	18,429,000	China
Polk	3,135,000	China
Red Willow	5,876,000	China
Richardson	4,687,000	China
Rock	556,000	China
Saline	4,667,000	China
Sarpy	17,981,000	China
Saunders	7,848,000	China
Scotts Bluff	14,454,000	China
Seward	6,230,000	China
Sheridan	2,605,000	China
Sherman	1,799,000	China
Sioux	211,000	China
Stanton	1,281,000	China
Thayer	4,642,000	China
Thomas	374,000	China
Thurston	2,255,000	China
Valley	2,266,000	China
Washington	5,765,000	China
Wayne	3,596,000	China
Webster	1,937,000	China
Wheeler	139,000	China
York	8,090,000	China
Nevada	$ 145,433,000	
Carson City	6,936,000	China
Churchill	2,329,000	China
Clark	79,560,000	China
Douglas	3,340,000	China
Elko	3,898,000	China
Esmeralda	81,000	China
Eureka	145,000	China
Humboldt	1,493,000	China
Lander	674,000	China
Lincoln	342,000	China
Lyon	2,151,000	China
Mineral	1,265,000	China
Nye	978,000	China
Pershing	521,000	China
Storey	122,000	China
Washoe	40,030,000	China
White Pine	1,568,000	China
New Hampshire	$ 281,147,000	
Belknap	10,480,000	Angola
Carroll	5,192,000	Angola
Cheshire	14,822,000	Cameroon
Coos	12,993,000	Cameroon
Grafton	14,293,000	Cameroon
Hillsborough	110,213,000	Cameroon
Merrimack	9,315,000	Cameroon
	5,604,000	Congo
	9,048,000	Equatorial Guinea
	2,643,000	Sao Tome and Principe
	100,000	St. Helena
Rockingham	29,594,000	Angola
	26,084,000	Congo
Strafford	19,660,000	Angola
Sullivan	11,106,000	Cameroon
New Jersey	$ 3,332,488,000	
Atlantic	60,443,000	India
Bergen	626,047,000	India
Burlington	108,211,000	India
Camden	179,359,000	India
Cape May	21,509,000	India

U.S. County	U.S. Church Resources Available for Global Word and Deed Mission (Dollars)	Nation
Cumberland	39,157,000	India
Essex	353,772,000	India
Gloucester	58,350,000	India
Hudson	279,152,000	India
Hunterdon	32,928,000	India
Mercer	127,915,000	India
Middlesex	294,216,000	India
Monmouth	192,769,000	India
Morris	184,225,000	India
Ocean	91,926,000	India
Passaic	166,586,000	India
Salem	15,139,000	India
Somerset	117,836,000	India
Sussex	31,534,000	India
Union	311,845,000	India
Warren	39,569,000	India
New Mexico	$ 441,812,000	
Bernalillo	147,881,000	Thailand
Catron	435,000	Thailand
Chaves	18,102,000	Thailand
Colfax	6,100,000	Thailand
Curry	18,243,000	Thailand
De Baca	1,359,000	Thailand
Dona Ana	21,596,000	Thailand
Eddy	22,209,000	Thailand
Grant	10,457,000	Thailand
Guadalupe	2,718,000	Thailand
Harding	805,000	Thailand
Hidalgo	2,257,000	Thailand
Lea	29,116,000	Thailand
Lincoln	3,044,000	Thailand
Los Alamos	11,812,000	Thailand
Luna	3,508,000	Thailand
McKinley	7,445,000	Thailand
Mora	1,789,000	Thailand
Otero	10,563,000	Thailand
Quay	5,307,000	Thailand
Rio Arriba	11,361,000	Thailand
Roosevelt	7,291,000	Thailand
Sandoval	8,154,000	Thailand
San Juan	18,299,000	Thailand
San Miguel	6,223,000	Thailand
Santa Fe	28,605,000	Thailand
Sierra	1,961,000	Thailand
Socorro	3,924,000	Thailand
Taos	9,661,000	Thailand
Torrance	1,873,000	Thailand
Union	2,407,000	Thailand
Valencia	17,307,000	Thailand
New York	$ 6,678,953,000	
Albany	915,000	Israel
	40,316,000	Jordan
	21,405,000	Portugal
	61,669,000	Romania
Allegany	8,772,000	Afghanistan
Bronx	4,010,000	Mauritania
	350,689,000	Morocco
	2,866,000	Western Sahara
Broome	23,747,000	Lebanon
	56,328,000	Syria
Cattaraugus	22,618,000	Pakistan
Cayuga	27,442,000	Turkey
Chautauqua	54,520,000	Pakistan
Chemung	33,777,000	Syria
Chenango	10,892,000	Syria
Clinton	27,814,000	Turkey
Columbia	13,778,000	Albania
	2,825,000	Egypt
Cortland	11,378,000	Turkey
Delaware	9,787,000	Lebanon

U.S. County	U.S. Church Resources Available for Global Word and Deed Mission (Dollars)	Nation	U.S. County	U.S. Church Resources Available for Global Word and Deed Mission (Dollars)	Nation
Dutchess	88,982,000	Egypt	Washington	14,229,000	Turkey
Erie	286,861,000	Afghanistan	Wayne	11,729,000	Turkey
	167,448,000	Iran		7,637,000	Yemen, South
	51,339,000	Pakistan	Westchester	573,863,000	Egypt
Essex	10,977,000	Turkey		25,664,000	Morocco
Franklin	16,893,000	Turkey	Wyoming	12,452,000	Afghanistan
Fulton	16,332,000	Turkey	Yates	1,190,000	Saudi Arabia
Genesee	24,813,000	Afghanistan		3,853,000	Yemen, South
Greene	9,805,000	Israel			
Hamilton	1,407,000	Turkey	North Carolina	$ 1,898,858,000	
Herkimer	23,644,000	Turkey	Alamance	33,907,000	India
Jefferson	27,747,000	Turkey	Alexander	8,810,000	India
Kings	231,936,000	Ghana	Alleghany	1,333,000	India
	159,542,000	Mali	Anson	10,638,000	India
	164,061,000	Upper Volta	Ashe	5,787,000	India
Lewis	7,316,000	Turkey	Avery	3,187,000	India
Livingston	108,000	Yemen, North	Beaufort	15,413,000	India
	12,622,000	Yemen, South	Bertie	4,633,000	India
Madison	17,719,000	Turkey	Bladen	9,917,000	India
Monroe	123,572,000	Afghanistan	Brunswick	7,383,000	India
	18,820,000	Iraq	Buncombe	57,107,000	India
	153,695,000	Yemen, North	Burke	25,079,000	India
Montgomery	22,282,000	Turkey	Cabarrus	41,442,000	India
Nassau	741,740,000	Nigeria	Caldwell	21,020,000	India
New York	8,175,000	Cape Verde	Camden	1,150,000	India
	17,256,000	Gambia	Carteret	9,341,000	India
	153,578,000	Guinea	Caswell	2,309,000	India
	23,181,000	Guinea-Bissau	Catawba	48,748,000	India
	38,354,000	Ivory Coast	Chatham	13,274,000	India
	44,023,000	Liberia	Cherokee	6,119,000	India
	41,745,000	Mauritania	Chowan	4,810,000	India
	148,065,000	Senegal	Clay	1,654,000	India
	97,278,000	Sierra Leone	Cleveland	32,068,000	India
Niagara	97,577,000	Iran	Columbus	14,715,000	India
Oneida	95,319,000	Turkey	Craven	20,678,000	India
Onondaga	181,633,000	Turkey	Cumberland	41,098,000	India
Ontario	26,833,000	Yemen, South	Currituck	2,365,000	India
Orange	89,679,000	Egypt	Dare	5,910,000	India
Orleans	13,359,000	Iraq	Davidson	33,737,000	India
Oswego	26,841,000	Turkey	Davie	7,683,000	India
Otsego	14,599,000	Syria	Duplin	8,822,000	India
Putnam	26,054,000	Egypt	Durham	49,121,000	India
Queens	94,501,000	Benin	Edgecombe	12,203,000	India
	48,376,000	Ghana	Forsyth	98,407,000	India
	402,530,000	Nigeria	Franklin	7,198,000	India
	61,713,000	Togo	Gaston	61,223,000	India
Rensselaer	48,431,000	Albania	Gates	2,580,000	India
	5,835,000	Portugal	Graham	2,539,000	India
Richmond	107,819,000	Ivory Coast	Granville	8,835,000	India
	43,331,000	Mali	Greene	3,139,000	India
Rockland	104,752,000	Egypt	Guilford	128,207,000	India
St. Lawrence	32,234,000	Turkey	Halifax	9,562,000	India
Saratoga	37,967,000	Turkey	Harnett	14,474,000	India
Schenectady	18,136,000	Jordan	Haywood	18,079,000	India
	71,622,000	Turkey	Henderson	21,389,000	India
Schoharie	5,352,000	Jordan	Hertford	4,788,000	India
Schuyler	4,949,000	Syria	Hoke	3,320,000	India
Seneca	9,110,000	Saudi Arabia	Hyde	1,127,000	India
Steuben	1,039,000	Bahrain	Iredell	31,940,000	India
	3,331,000	Kuwait	Jackson	7,238,000	India
	2,467,000	Oman	Johnston	17,848,000	India
	569,000	Qatar	Jones	1,820,000	India
	14,514,000	Saudi Arabia	Lee	14,630,000	India
	397,000	Syria	Lenoir	15,037,000	India
	2,198,000	United Arab Emirates	Lincoln	15,325,000	India
Suffolk	147,276,000	Niger	McDowell	10,504,000	India
	341,885,000	Nigeria	Macon	7,513,000	India
Sullivan	13,747,000	Egypt	Madison	5,250,000	India
Tioga	10,139,000	Syria	Martin	8,172,000	India
Tompkins	15,322,000	Syria	Mecklenburg	194,744,000	India
Ulster	54,705,000	Egypt	Mitchell	5,499,000	India
Warren	15,331,000	Turkey	Montgomery	7,434,000	India

U.S. County	U.S. Church Resources Available for Global Word and Deed Mission (Dollars)	Nation
Moore	10,726,000	India
Nash	19,068,000	India
New Hanover	45,903,000	India
Northampton	3,416,000	India
Onslow	13,348,000	India
Orange	19,924,000	India
Pamlico	1,829,000	India
Pasquotank	9,996,000	India
Pender	4,125,000	India
Perquimans	2,689,000	India
Person	6,712,000	India
Pitt	13,861,000	India
Polk	6,800,000	India
Randolph	24,566,000	India
Richmond	14,680,000	India
Robeson	20,569,000	India
Rockingham	19,407,000	India
Rowan	40,788,000	India
Rutherford	22,725,000	India
Sampson	17,352,000	India
Scotland	8,836,000	India
Stanly	19,811,000	India
Stokes	6,524,000	India
Surry	18,292,000	India
Swain	2,561,000	India
Transylvania	7,557,000	India
Tyrrell	1,309,000	India
Union	25,353,000	India
Vance	10,253,000	India
Wake	110,023,000	India
Warren	3,277,000	India
Washington	4,401,000	India
Watauga	7,501,000	India
Wayne	18,609,000	India
Wilkes	19,969,000	India
Wilson	13,531,000	India
Yadkin	10,244,000	India
Yancey	3,041,000	India
North Dakota	$ 313,205,000	
Adams	1,919,000	China
Barnes	6,367,000	China
Benson	3,984,000	China
Billings	338,000	China
Bottineau	4,891,000	China
Bowman	2,275,000	China
Burke	2,231,000	China
Burleigh	30,142,000	China
Cass	46,033,000	China
Cavalier	3,526,000	China
Dickey	2,853,000	China
Divide	1,702,000	China
Dunn	2,724,000	China
Eddy	1,520,000	China
Emmons	2,841,000	China
Foster	2,539,000	China
Golden Valley	1,511,000	China
Grand Forks	23,731,000	China
Grant	1,714,000	China
Griggs	1,397,000	China
Hettinger	2,434,000	China
Kidder	1,429,000	China
La Moore	2,983,000	China
Logan	1,487,000	China
McHenry	4,303,000	China
McIntosh	2,816,000	China
McKenzie	2,608,000	China
McLean	6,375,000	China
Mercer	4,551,000	China
Morton	12,799,000	China
Mountrail	3,133,000	China
Nelson	3,086,000	China
Oliver	845,000	China
Pembina	5,258,000	China
Pierce	2,902,000	China
Ramsey	7,433,000	China
Ransom	3,279,000	China
Renville	1,890,000	China
Richland	8,255,000	China
Rolette	6,483,000	China
Sargent	2,297,000	China
Sheridan	1,151,000	China
Sioux	1,663,000	China
Slope	216,000	China
Stark	11,772,000	China
Steele	1,321,000	China
Stutsman	10,938,000	China
Towner	2,180,000	China
Traill	5,521,000	China
Walsh	5,869,000	China
Ward	22,960,000	China
Wells	4,807,000	China
Williams	13,923,000	China
Ohio	$ 3,887,545,000	
Adams	3,638,000	China
Allen	40,181,000	China
Ashland	13,883,000	China
Ashtabula	31,420,000	China
Athens	6,571,000	China
Auglaize	18,740,000	China
Belmont	28,417,000	China
Brown	7,377,000	China
Butler	74,446,000	China
Carroll	5,470,000	China
Champaign	7,084,000	China
Clark	39,524,000	China
Clermont	27,221,000	China
Clinton	10,050,000	China
Columbiana	35,613,000	China
Coshocton	10,675,000	China
Crawford	19,616,000	China
Cuyahoga	824,929,000	China
Darke	15,744,000	China
Defiance	19,050,000	China
Delaware	9,669,000	China
Erie	32,759,000	China
Fairfield	25,213,000	China
Fayette	5,495,000	China
Franklin	252,325,000	China
Fulton	16,909,000	China
Gallia	4,029,000	China
Geauga	24,652,000	China
Greene	26,090,000	China
Guernsey	10,035,000	China
Hamilton	381,757,000	China
Hancock	23,331,000	China
Hardin	8,585,000	China
Harrison	4,435,000	China
Henry	14,188,000	China
Highland	6,559,000	China
Hocking	4,326,000	China
Holmes	8,094,000	China
Huron	19,542,000	China
Jackson	4,262,000	China
Jefferson	32,613,000	China
Knox	12,328,000	China
Lake	87,615,000	China
Lawrence	7,838,000	China
Licking	31,393,000	China
Logan	11,632,000	China
Lorain	106,189,000	China
Lucas	186,555,000	China
Madison	8,596,000	China

U.S. County	U.S. Church Resources Available for Global Word and Deed Mission (Dollars)	Nation
Mahoning	131,596,000	China
Marion	19,950,000	China
Medina	40,585,000	China
Meigs	4,056,000	China
Mercer	18,510,000	China
Miami	27,191,000	China
Monroe	4,547,000	China
Montgomery	185,468,000	China
Morgan	4,261,000	China
Morrow	4,361,000	China
Muskingum	24,063,000	China
Noble	2,579,000	China
Ottawa	16,949,000	China
Paulding	6,699,000	China
Perry	6,656,000	China
Pickaway	8,701,000	China
Pike	2,187,000	China
Portage	24,555,000	China
Preble	9,074,000	China
Putnam	17,393,000	China
Richland	38,534,000	China
Ross	11,416,000	China
Sandusky	25,116,000	China
Scioto	11,338,000	China
Seneca	29,385,000	China
Shelby	15,932,000	China
Stark	129,486,000	China
Summit	195,573,000	China
Trumbull	92,732,000	China
Tuscarawas	30,244,000	China
Union	7,682,000	China
Van Wert	10,592,000	China
Vinton	887,000	China
Warren	19,361,000	China
Washington	15,496,000	China
Wayne	33,291,000	China
Williams	13,070,000	China
Wood	31,111,000	China
Wyandot	10,255,000	China
Oklahoma	$ 1,221,776,000	
Adair	2,940,000	China
Alfalfa	3,505,000	China
Atoka	2,744,000	China
Beaver	3,554,000	China
Beckham	8,404,000	China
Blaine	5,048,000	China
Bryan	9,351,000	China
Caddo	14,917,000	China
Canadian	16,780,000	China
Carter	20,651,000	China
Cherokee	4,995,000	China
Choctaw	4,873,000	China
Cimarron	4,595,000	China
Cleveland	30,214,000	China
Coal	1,469,000	China
Comanche	29,837,000	China
Cotton	3,665,000	China
Craig	6,924,000	China
Creek	19,470,000	China
Custer	11,513,000	China
Delaware	3,967,000	China
Dewey	3,262,000	China
Ellis	2,780,000	China
Garfield	31,220,000	China
Garvin	12,692,000	China
Grady	14,533,000	China
Grant	5,305,000	China
Greer	3,711,000	China
Harmon	2,914,000	China
Harper	3,360,000	China
Haskell	2,719,000	China
Hughes	5,179,000	China
Jackson	10,379,000	China
Jefferson	3,580,000	China
Johnston	2,521,000	China
Kay	31,379,000	China
Kingfisher	9,033,000	China
Kiowa	5,499,000	China
Latimer	2,186,000	China
Le Flore	9,082,000	China
Lincoln	7,516,000	China
Logan	3,651,000	China
Love	2,653,000	China
McClain	9,274,000	China
McCurtain	6,748,000	China
McIntosh	3,380,000	China
Major	3,539,000	China
Marshall	3,011,000	China
Mayes	9,665,000	China
Murray	4,048,000	China
Muskogee	26,390,000	China
Noble	4,872,000	China
Nowata	3,746,000	China
Okfuskee	2,667,000	China
Oklahoma	300,587,000	China
Okmulgee	12,286,000	China
Osage	8,536,000	China
Ottawa	14,013,000	China
Pawnee	4,925,000	China
Payne	14,013,000	China
Pittsburg	12,205,000	China
Pontotoc	13,403,000	China
Pottawatomie	21,268,000	China
Pushmataha	2,310,000	China
Roger Mills	2,181,000	China
Rogers	12,470,000	China
Seminole	10,867,000	China
Sequoyah	4,573,000	China
Stephens	23,525,000	China
Texas	15,120,000	China
Tillman	6,698,000	China
Tulsa	224,806,000	China
Wagoner	4,134,000	China
Washington	32,925,000	China
Washita	5,802,000	China
Woods	5,117,000	China
Woodward	8,102,000	China
Oregon	$ 625,236,000	
Baker	303,000	Hong Kong
	2,714,000	Macao
Benton	11,775,000	Philippines
Clackamas	26,196,000	China (Taiwan)
	20,334,000	Korea, South
Clatsop	5,200,000	Korea, South
Columbia	6,244,000	Korea, South
Coos	9,381,000	Philippines
Crook	2,052,000	China (Taiwan)
Curry	2,515,000	Philippines
Deschutes	9,429,000	China (Taiwan)
Douglas	15,714,000	Philippines
Gilliam	448,000	China (Taiwan)
Grant	968,000	China (Taiwan)
Harney	1,409,000	China (Taiwan)
Hood River	4,316,000	China (Taiwan)
Jackson	25,878,000	Philippines
Jefferson	2,285,000	China (Taiwan)
Josephine	7,308,000	Philippines
Klamath	11,737,000	Philippines
Lake	1,292,000	Philippines
Lane	47,895,000	Philippines
Lincoln	5,108,000	Philippines
Linn	17,746,000	Philippines

U.S. County	U.S. Church Resources Available for Global Word and Deed Mission (Dollars)	Nation
Malheur	4,857,000	China (Taiwan)
Marion	56,757,000	China (Taiwan)
	16,539,000	Philippines
Morrow	1,631,000	China (Taiwan)
Multnomah	187,364,000	Korea, South
Polk	12,439,000	Philippines
Sherman	618,000	China (Taiwan)
Tillamook	3,325,000	Korea, South
Umatilla	8,465,000	China (Taiwan)
	3,970,000	Hong Kong
Union	3,837,000	Hong Kong
Wallowa	1,317,000	Hong Kong
Wasco	5,277,000	China (Taiwan)
Washington	67,515,000	Korea, South
Wheeler	179,000	China (Taiwan)
Yamhill	12,899,000	Korea, South
Pennsylvania	$ 5,189,673,000	
Adams	24,099,000	India
Allegheny	896,679,000	Pakistan
Armstrong	35,361,000	Pakistan
Beaver	91,530,000	Pakistan
Bedford	12,409,000	India
Berks	142,419,000	India
Blair	46,738,000	Pakistan
Bradford	15,797,000	Pakistan
Bucks	211,051,000	India
Butler	60,436,000	Pakistan
Cambria	97,178,000	Pakistan
Cameron	2,391,000	Pakistan
Carbon	27,946,000	India
Centre	28,655,000	Pakistan
Chester	128,305,000	India
Clarion	13,604,000	Pakistan
Clearfield	28,649,000	Pakistan
Clinton	11,258,000	Pakistan
Columbia	22,675,000	India
Crawford	23,903,000	Pakistan
Cumberland	73,127,000	India
Dauphin	91,111,000	India
Delaware	306,785,000	India
Elk	18,337,000	Pakistan
Erie	106,816,000	Pakistan
Fayette	56,327,000	Pakistan
Forest	1,034,000	Pakistan
Franklin	31,533,000	India
Fulton	2,470,000	India
Greene	10,977,000	Pakistan
Huntingdon	10,194,000	India
Indiana	27,413,000	Pakistan
Jefferson	19,405,000	Pakistan
Juniata	6,876,000	India
Lackawanna	107,940,000	India
Lancaster	144,123,000	India
Lawrence	44,520,000	Pakistan
Lebanon	41,062,000	India
Lehigh	133,118,000	India
Luzerne	161,738,000	India
Lycoming	41,921,000	Pakistan
McKean	18,742,000	Pakistan
Mercer	53,324,000	Pakistan
Mifflin	14,998,000	India
Monroe	19,044,000	India
Montgomery	387,313,000	India
Montour	6,238,000	Pakistan
Northampton	119,181,000	India
Northumberland	44,356,000	Pakistan
Perry	9,742,000	India
Philadelphia	536,780,000	India
Pike	2,929,000	India
Potter	3,093,000	Pakistan
Schuylkill	85,745,000	India

U.S. County	U.S. Church Resources Available for Global Word and Deed Mission (Dollars)	Nation
Snyder	9,146,000	Pakistan
Somerset	19,951,000	India
	14,162,000	Pakistan
Sullivan	1,589,000	Pakistan
Susquehanna	8,928,000	Pakistan
Tioga	8,912,000	Pakistan
Union	8,228,000	Pakistan
Venango	22,551,000	Pakistan
Warren	17,756,000	Pakistan
Washington	88,336,000	Pakistan
Wayne	10,752,000	India
Westmoreland	188,238,000	Pakistan
Wyoming	5,570,000	India
York	126,159,000	India
Rhode Island	$ 512,430,000	
Bristol	30,001,000	Kenya
Kent	84,769,000	Somalia
Newport	36,156,000	Kenya
Providence	292,723,000	Kenya
	39,061,000	Somalia
Washington	8,990,000	Djibouti
	9,009,000	Ethiopa
	11,721,000	Somalia
South Carolina	$ 890,301,000	
Abbeville	6,658,000	India
Aiken	37,465,000	India
Allendale	2,090,000	India
Anderson	44,108,000	India
Bamberg	3,800,000	India
Barnwell	5,847,000	India
Beaufort	10,685,000	India
Berkeley	11,164,000	India
Calhoun	2,094,000	India
Charleston	72,579,000	India
Cherokee	16,581,000	India
Chester	13,802,000	India
Chesterfield	14,799,000	India
Clarendon	2,957,000	India
Colleton	7,697,000	India
Darlington	12,921,000	India
Dillon	5,468,000	India
Dorchester	15,170,000	India
Edgefield	3,659,000	India
Fairfield	4,810,000	India
Florence	25,574,000	India
Georgetown	7,278,000	India
Greenville	111,846,000	India
Greenwood	18,739,000	India
Hampton	4,709,000	India
Horry	23,728,000	India
Jasper	1,883,000	India
Kershaw	15,633,000	India
Lancaster	22,764,000	India
Laurens	16,205,000	India
Lee	2,368,000	India
Lexington	42,162,000	India
McCormick	1,215,000	India
Marion	5,569,000	India
Marlboro	6,172,000	India
Newberry	11,774,000	India
Oconee	14,462,000	India
Orangeburg	17,691,000	India
Pickens	20,562,000	India
Richland	70,443,000	India
Saluda	4,505,000	India
Spartanburg	77,683,000	India
Sumter	16,822,000	India
Union	10,562,000	India
Williamsburg	5,599,000	India
York	39,999,000	India

U.S. County	U.S. Church Resources Available for Global Word and Deed Mission (Dollars)	Nation	U.S. County	U.S. Church Resources Available for Global Word and Deed Mission (Dollars)	Nation
			Bledsoe	1,085,000	India
South Dakota	$ 273,902,000		Blount	30,527,000	Nepal
Aurora	1,385,000	China	Bradley	20,555,000	India
Beadle	9,308,000	China	Campbell	7,196,000	Nepal
Bennett	520,000	China	Cannon	2,500,000	India
Bon Homme	3,677,000	China	Carroll	7,921,000	India
Brookings	7,653,000	China	Carter	11,415,000	Nepal
Brown	17,720,000	China	Cheatham	3,048,000	India
Brule	2,448,000	China	Chester	2,649,000	India
Buffalo	298,000	China	Claiborne	7,480,000	Nepal
Butte	1,773,000	China	Clay	1,037,000	India
Campbell	1,137,000	China	Cocke	6,235,000	Nepal
Charles Mix	3,340,000	China	Coffee	11,182,000	India
Clark	2,151,000	China	Crockett	5,234,000	India
Clay	3,267,000	China	Cumberland	4,641,000	Nepal
Codington	9,772,000	China	Davidson	193,959,000	India
Corson	1,547,000	China	Decatur	2,569,000	India
Custer	939,000	China	De Kalb	3,525,000	India
Davison	8,655,000	China	Dickson	6,601,000	India
Day	3,631,000	China	Dyer	3,330,000	Bhutan
Deuel	2,097,000	China		8,752,000	India
Dewey	1,569,000	China	Fayette	5,652,000	India
Douglas	1,932,000	China	Fentress	1,485,000	Nepal
Edmunds	2,327,000	China	Franklin	9,056,000	India
Fall River	2,700,000	China	Gibson	18,081,000	India
Faulk	1,864,000	China	Giles	7,740,000	India
Grant	4,589,000	China	Grainger	5,060,000	Nepal
Gregory	2,313,000	China	Greene	12,986,000	Nepal
Haakon	1,266,000	China	Grundy	1,623,000	India
Hamlin	1,945,000	China	Hamblen	14,280,000	Nepal
Hand	2,062,000	China	Hamilton	102,570,000	India
Hanson	890,000	China	Hancock	2,699,000	Nepal
Harding	598,000	China	Hardeman	5,719,000	India
Hughes	5,978,000	China	Hardin	5,182,000	India
Hutchinson	3,980,000	China	Hawkins	11,043,000	Nepal
Hyde	1,009,000	China	Haywood	5,612,000	India
Jackson	653,000	China	Henderson	4,154,000	India
Jerauld	1,022,000	China	Henry	10,899,000	Bhutan
Jones	487,000	China	Hickman	3,294,000	India
Kingsbury	3,486,000	China	Houston	1,720,000	India
Lake	4,083,000	China	Humphreys	4,545,000	India
Lawrence	5,168,000	China	Jackson	1,237,000	India
Lincoln	4,460,000	China	Jefferson	9,988,000	Nepal
Lyman	1,242,000	China	Johnson	4,147,000	Nepal
McCook	2,745,000	China	Knox	128,501,000	Nepal
McPherson	2,117,000	China	Lake	1,926,000	Bhutan
Marshall	2,755,000	China	Lauderdale	5,420,000	India
Meade	3,027,000	China	Lawrence	11,575,000	India
Mellette	574,000	China	Lewis	1,387,000	India
Miner	1,688,000	China	Lincoln	8,298,000	India
Minnehaha	55,291,000	China	Loudon	11,263,000	Nepal
Moody	2,514,000	China	McMinn	16,451,000	India
Pennington	23,809,000	China	McNairy	5,611,000	India
Perkins	1,969,000	China	Macon	1,163,000	India
Potter	2,274,000	China	Madison	31,382,000	India
Roberts	4,155,000	China	Marion	5,098,000	India
Sanborn	1,178,000	China	Marshall	6,042,000	India
Shannon	1,579,000	China	Maury	13,829,000	India
Spink	3,481,000	China	Meigs	1,897,000	India
Stanley	252,000	China	Monroe	8,800,000	Nepal
Sully	1,151,000	China	Montgomery	18,670,000	India
Todd	1,420,000	China	Moore	935,000	India
Tripp	2,728,000	China	Morgan	2,485,000	Nepal
Turner	5,793,000	China	Obion	12,868,000	Bhutan
Union	4,318,000	China	Overton	3,100,000	India
Walworth	3,738,000	China	Perry	1,134,000	India
Yankton	7,662,000	China	Pickett	520,000	India
Ziebach	743,000	China	Polk	2,901,000	India
				3,261,000	Nepal
Tennessee	$ 1,452,372,000		Putnam	11,099,000	India
Anderson	33,995,000	Nepal	Rhea	6,393,000	India
Bedford	8,826,000	India	Roane	12,388,000	Nepal
Benton	3,387,000	India			

U.S. County	U.S. Church Resources Available for Global Word and Deed Mission (Dollars)	Nation	U.S. County	U.S. Church Resources Available for Global Word and Deed Mission (Dollars)	Nation
Robertson	12,573,000	India	Coleman	4,618,000	Burma
Rutherford	19,786,000	India	Collin	45,556,000	Bangladesh
Scott	3,506,000	Nepal	Collingsworth	2,137,000	Thailand
Sequatchie	1,382,000	India	Colorado	8,399,000	Ecuador
Sevier	13,729,000	Nepal	Comal	15,356,000	Cuba
Shelby	255,823,000	India	Comanche	4,342,000	Burma
Smith	2,762,000	India	Concho	808,000	Mexico
Stewart	2,864,000	India	Cooke	11,975,000	Burma
Sullivan	46,330,000	Nepal	Coryell	6,900,000	Haiti
Sumner	19,501,000	India	Cottle	2,393,000	Burma
Tipton	9,451,000	India	Crane	2,208,000	Mexico
Trousdale	924,000	India	Crockett	2,934,000	Mexico
Unicoi	4,571,000	Nepal	Crosby	4,696,000	Thailand
Union	1,612,000	Nepal	Culberson	1,758,000	Mexico
Van Buren	719,000	India	Dallam	7,517,000	Thailand
Warren	8,798,000	India	Dallas	501,585,000	Bangladesh
Washington	26,843,000	Nepal		206,417,000	Burma
Wayne	2,755,000	India	Dawson	8,505,000	Burma
Weakley	10,457,000	Bhutan	Deaf Smith	9,626,000	Thailand
White	3,812,000	India	Delta	2,121,000	Bangladesh
Williamson	16,885,000	India	Denton	34,221,000	Burma
Wilson	16,471,000	India	De Witt	7,135,000	Peru
			Dickens	1,734,000	Burma
Texas	$ 5,473,321,000		Dimmit	3,595,000	Mexico
Anderson	12,761,000	Bangladesh	Donley	2,480,000	Thailand
Andrews	6,154,000	Mexico	Duval	1,895,000	Bolivia
Angelina	23,465,000	Bangladesh	Eastland	8,373,000	Burma
Aransas	4,080,000	Brazil	Ector	54,831,000	Mexico
Archer	3,773,000	Burma	Edwards	1,156,000	Guatemala
Armstrong	1,507,000	Thailand	Ellis	22,973,000	Bangladesh
Atascosa	8,509,000	Bolivia	El Paso	101,800,000	Mexico
Austin	5,771,000	Ecuador	Erath	9,399,000	Burma
Bailey	4,792,000	Thailand	Falls	7,232,000	Colombia
Bandera	2,042,000	Guatemala	Fannin	9,156,000	Bangladesh
Bastrop	4,769,000	Haiti	Fayette	9,619,000	Peru
Baylor	4,357,000	Burma	Fisher	3,195,000	Burma
Bee	8,144,000	Brazil	Floyd	6,267,000	Burma
Bell	38,199,000	Haiti	Foard	1,779,000	Burma
Bexar	21,110,000	Costa Rica	Fort Bend	32,971,000	Brazil
	8,393,000	Cuba	Franklin	2,324,000	Bangladesh
	100,584,000	El Salvador	Freestone	4,823,000	Colombia
	93,126,000	Guatemala	Frio	3,352,000	Bolivia
	82,910,000	Honduras	Gaines	5,021,000	Thailand
	55,087,000	Nicaragua	Galveston	74,151,000	Brazil
	17,504,000	Panama	Garza	2,192,000	Burma
Blanco	1,756,000	Haiti	Gillespie	6,921,000	Cuba
Borden	402,000	Burma	Glasscock	1,116,000	Mexico
Bosque	7,321,000	Dominican Republic	Goliad	2,348,000	Brazil
Bowie	28,543,000	Bangladesh	Gonzales	6,641,000	Peru
Brazoria	63,293,000	Brazil	Gray	17,622,000	Thailand
Brazos	17,823,000	Colombia	Grayson	40,417,000	Bangladesh
Brewster	2,208,000	Mexico	Gregg	44,917,000	Bangladesh
Briscoe	2,069,000	Thailand	Grimes	5,624,000	Colombia
Brooks	2,922,000	Brazil	Guadalupe	12,796,000	Cuba
Brown	13,217,000	Burma	Hale	19,154,000	Thailand
Burleson	2,707,000	Colombia	Hall	2,686,000	Thailand
Burnet	6,739,000	Haiti	Hamilton	3,185,000	Dominican Republic
Caldwell	5,219,000	Haiti	Hansford	4,811,000	Thailand
Calhoun	13,140,000	Brazil	Hardeman	3,231,000	Burma
Callahan	3,959,000	Burma	Hardin	12,389,000	Bangladesh
Cameron	20,103,000	Argentina	Harris	216,865,000	Brazil
	42,399,000	Paraguay		353,807,000	Colombia
Camp	4,495,000	Bangladesh		110,007,000	Ecuador
Carson	5,762,000	Thailand		271,628,000	Peru
Cass	11,847,000	Bangladesh	Harrison	17,237,000	Bangladesh
Castro	3,306,000	Thailand	Hartley	461,000	Thailand
Chambers	5,811,000	Brazil	Haskell	5,145,000	Burma
Cherokee	16,277,000	Bangladesh	Hays	8,603,000	Cuba
Childress	3,585,000	Thailand	Hemphill	2,677,000	Thailand
Clay	4,396,000	Burma	Henderson	10,458,000	Bangladesh
Cochran	2,224,000	Thailand	Hidalgo	14,121,000	Argentina
Coke	1,432,000	Mexico		54,669,000	Chile

U.S. County	U.S. Church Resources Available for Global Word and Deed Mission (Dollars)	Nation
Hill	8,667,000	Dominican Republic
Hockley	9,392,000	Thailand
Hood	4,352,000	Burma
Hopkins	9,354,000	Bangladesh
Houston	5,939,000	Bangladesh
Howard	18,663,000	Mexico
Hudspeth	1,492,000	Mexico
Hunt	20,117,000	Bangladesh
Hutchinson	16,115,000	Thailand
Irion	461,000	Mexico
Jack	3,782,000	Burma
Jackson	5,362,000	Brazil
Jasper	11,044,000	Bangladesh
Jeff Davis	1,173,000	Mexico
Jefferson	19,272,000	Bangladesh
	118,302,000	Brazil
Jim Hogg	2,385,000	Bolivia
Jim Wells	12,398,000	Bolivia
Johnson	25,639,000	Burma
Jones	9,278,000	Burma
Karnes	6,631,000	Peru
Kaufman	15,095,000	Bangladesh
Kendall	4,353,000	Cuba
Kenedy	626,000	Brazil
Kent	450,000	Burma
Kerr	10,056,000	Cuba
Kimble	1,457,000	Mexico
King	107,000	Burma
Kinney	852,000	Mexico
Kleberg	11,605,000	Brazil
Knox	4,253,000	Burma
Lamar	13,450,000	Bangladesh
Lamb	8,384,000	Thailand
Lampasas	3,172,000	Dominican Republic
	232,000	Haiti
La Salle	1,981,000	Bolivia
Lavaca	8,563,000	Peru
Lee	4,461,000	Haiti
Leon	3,449,000	Colombia
Liberty	18,509,000	Brazil
Limestone	5,497,000	Colombia
Lipscomb	2,760,000	Thailand
Live Oak	2,725,000	Brazil
Llano	3,412,000	Haiti
Loving	0,000	Mexico
Lubbock	29,747,000	Burma
	54,742,000	Thailand
Lynn	3,414,000	Burma
McCulloch	3,258,000	Mexico
McLennan	149,000	Anguilla
	1,108,000	Antigua
	10,685,000	Colombia
	1,813,000	Dominica
	63,634,000	Dominican Republic
	2,302,000	Grenada
	162,000	Montserrat
	923,000	St. Kitts-Nevis
	2,404,000	St. Lucia
	2,436,000	St. Vincent
McMullen	405,000	Bolivia
Madison	2,478,000	Colombia
Marion	2,161,000	Bangladesh
Martin	2,654,000	Mexico
Mason	1,456,000	Mexico
Matagorda	13,622,000	Brazil
Maverick	4,106,000	Mexico
Medina	9,562,000	Guatemala
Menard	1,313,000	Mexico
Midland	48,169,000	Mexico
Milam	9,383,000	Haiti
Mills	2,691,000	Dominican Republic
Mitchell	4,870,000	Burma

U.S. County	U.S. Church Resources Available for Global Word and Deed Mission (Dollars)	Nation
Montague	6,414,000	Burma
Montgomery	18,206,000	Brazil
	16,593,000	Guyana
Moore	7,039,000	Thailand
Morris	7,147,000	Bangladesh
Motley	1,246,000	Burma
Nacogdoches	12,407,000	Bangladesh
Navarro	14,796,000	Bangladesh
Newton	2,614,000	Bangladesh
Nolan	9,429,000	Burma
Nueces	83,921,000	Bolivia
	18,180,000	Brazil
Ochiltree	5,416,000	Thailand
Oldham	2,660,000	Thailand
Orange	37,421,000	Bangladesh
Palo Pinto	9,891,000	Burma
Panola	6,561,000	Bangladesh
Parker	13,991,000	Burma
Parmer	5,722,000	Thailand
Pecos	6,750,000	Mexico
Polk	6,211,000	Brazil
Potter	67,751,000	Thailand
Presidio	2,447,000	Mexico
Rains	1,688,000	Bangladesh
Randall	20,351,000	Thailand
Reagan	2,274,000	Mexico
Real	819,000	Guatemala
Red River	4,597,000	Bangladesh
Reeves	6,469,000	Mexico
Refugio	4,435,000	Brazil
Roberts	1,559,000	Thailand
Robertson	3,413,000	Colombia
Rockwall	5,320,000	Bangladesh
Runnels	6,409,000	Mexico
Rusk	14,318,000	Bangladesh
	2,371,000	Bangladesh
Sabine	1,791,000	Bangladesh
San Augustine	1,576,000	Brazil
San Jacinto	20,537,000	Brazil
San Patricio	2,254,000	Mexico
San Saba	1,226,000	Mexico
Schleicher	10,556,000	Burma
Scurry	2,200,000	Burma
Shackelford	6,812,000	Bangladesh
Shelby	2,776,000	Thailand
Sherman	56,404,000	Bangladesh
Smith	1,576,000	Burma
Somervell	10,439,000	Argentina
Starr	3,839,000	Burma
Stephens	566,000	Mexico
Sterling	865,000	Burma
Stonewall	2,262,000	Mexico
Sutton	7,545,000	Thailand
Swisher	338,129,000	Burma
Tarrant	53,806,000	Burma
Taylor	1,125,000	Mexico
Terrell	6,883,000	Thailand
Terry	2,668,000	Burma
Throckmorton	9,860,000	Bangladesh
Titus	31,231,000	Mexico
Tom Green	66,653,000	Cuba
Travis	36,651,000	Haiti
	37,703,000	Jamaica
	78,000	Turks and Caicos Islands
Trinity	2,196,000	Brazil
Tyler	4,988,000	Bangladesh
Upshur	8,145,000	Bangladesh
Upton	2,725,000	Mexico
Uvalde	7,570,000	Guatemala
Val Verde	9,434,000	Mexico
Van Zandt	11,146,000	Bangladesh

U.S. County	U.S. Church Resources Available for Global Word and Deed Mission (Dollars)	Nation	U.S. County	U.S. Church Resources Available for Global Word and Deed Mission (Dollars)	Nation
Victoria	31,973,000	Brazil	Virginia[3]	$ 1,572,040,000	
Walker	6,523,000	Brazil	Accomack	8,488,000	India
Waller	3,828,000	Peru	Albemarle	26,727,000	India
Ward	6,800,000	Mexico	Alleghany	9,611,000	India
Washington	9,870,000	Peru	Amelia	1,481,000	India
Webb	14,005,000	Argentina	Amherst	5,556,000	India
	8,554,000	Bolivia	Appomattox	3,778,000	India
	1,090,000	Mexico	Arlington	156,568,000	India
Wharton	17,373,000	Brazil	Augusta	33,718,000	India
Wheeler	4,535,000	Thailand	Bath	1,705,000	India
Wichita	57,609,000	Burma	Bedford	13,037,000	India
Wilbarger	8,302,000	Burma	Bland	1,337,000	India
Willacy	8,615,000	Brazil	Botetourt	5,543,000	India
Williamson	17,915,000	Haiti	Brunswick	3,152,000	India
Wilson	4,316,000	Peru	Buchanan	3,743,000	India
Winkler	5,918,000	Mexico	Buckingham	2,416,000	India
Wise	8,064,000	Burma	Campbell	37,513,000	India
Wood	10,287,000	Bangladesh	Caroline	2,919,000	India
Yoakum	4,758,000	Thailand	Carroll	7,227,000	India
Young	10,758,000	Burma	Charles City	977,000	India
Zapata	1,083,000	Argentina	Charlotte	3,270,000	India
Zavala	2,409,000	Belize	Chesterfield	26,888,000	India
	1,718,000	Bolivia	Clarke	2,351,000	India
			Craig	862,000	India
Utah	$ 69,987,000		Culpeper	5,703,000	India
Beaver	50,000	China	Cumberland	799,000	India
Box Elder	1,485,000	China	Dickenson	1,123,000	India
Cache	1,131,000	China	Dinwiddie	23,237,000	India
Carbon	3,806,000	China	Essex	1,759,000	India
Daggett	11,000	China	Fairfax	222,998,000	India
Davis	6,556,000	China	Fauquier	9,138,000	India
Duchesne	495,000	China	Floyd	1,897,000	India
Emery	45,000	China	Fluvanna	2,534,000	India
Garfield	8,000	China	Franklin	7,000,000	India
Grand	1,171,000	China	Frederick	15,956,000	India
Iron	270,000	China	Giles	5,057,000	India
Juab	76,000	China	Gloucester	5,344,000	India
Kane	71,000	China	Goochland	2,828,000	India
Millard	24,000	China	Grayson	4,047,000	India
Morgan	953,000	China	Greene	1,097,000	India
Piute	2,000	China	Greensville	3,453,000	India
Rich	3,000	China	Halifax	10,812,000	India
Salt Lake	37,321,000	China	Hampton City	27,975,000	India
San Juan	299,000	China	Hanover	18,075,000	India
Sanpete	64,000	China	Henrico	180,530,000	India
Sevier	285,000	China	Henry	18,498,000	India
Summit	265,000	China	Highland	979,000	India
Tooele	1,781,000	China	Isle of Wight	3,931,000	India
Uintah	1,357,000	China	James City	7,270,000	India
Utah	1,979,000	China	King and Queen	1,359,000	India
Wasatch	25,000	China	King George	3,952,000	India
Washington	234,000	China	King William	3,211,000	India
Wayne	2,000	China	Lancaster	3,917,000	India
Weber	10,218,000	China	Lee	5,876,000	India
			Loudoun	18,772,000	India
Vermont	$ 144,736,000		Louisa	3,759,000	India
Addison	6,797,000	Chad	Lunenberg	2,869,000	India
Bennington	10,067,000	Central African Republic	Madison	1,881,000	India
Caledonia	5,489,000	Cameroon	Mathews	2,603,000	India
	120,000	Chad	Mecklenburg	7,430,000	India
Chittenden	42,731,000	Chad	Middlesex	2,176,000	India
Essex	1,052,000	Cameroon	Montgomery	11,618,000	India
Franklin	12,089,000	Chad	Nelson	3,871,000	India
Grand Isle	1,798,000	Chad	New Kent	1,228,000	India
Lamoille	3,223,000	Chad	Newport News City	39,168,000	India
Orange	3,379,000	Chad	Norfolk City	111,945,000	India
Orleans	5,338,000	Chad	Northampton	2,485,000	India
Rutland	18,053,000	Chad	Northumberland	3,056,000	India
Washington	15,919,000	Chad	Nottoway	3,176,000	India
Windham	2,010,000	Central African Republic	Orange	5,800,000	India
	5,510,000	Chad	Page	4,840,000	India
Windsor	11,161,000	Chad	Patrick	2,268,000	India

U.S. County	U.S. Church Resources Available for Global Word and Deed Mission (Dollars)	Nation	U.S. County	U.S. Church Resources Available for Global Word and Deed Mission (Dollars)	Nation
Pittsylvania	25,376,000	India	Yakima	44,122,000	Korea, South
Powhatan	1,819,000	India			
Prince Edward	3,211,000	India	West Virginia	$ 464,954,000	
Prince George	7,760,000	India	Barbour	3,297,000	India
Prince William	42,446,000	India	Berkeley	12,860,000	India
Pulaski	7,681,000	India	Boone	4,405,000	China
Rappahannock	1,460,000	India	Braxton	1,865,000	China
Richmond	3,216,000	India	Brooke	9,418,000	India
Roanoke	76,129,000	India	Cabell	32,080,000	China
Rockbridge	8,073,000	India	Calhoun	1,254,000	China
Rockingham	21,293,000	India	Clay	1,294,000	China
Russell	3,345,000	India	Doddridge	1,239,000	India
Scott	3,335,000	India	Fayette	10,229,000	China
Shenandoah	10,190,000	India	Gilmer	1,045,000	China
Smyth	6,922,000	India	Grant	2,821,000	India
Southampton	9,548,000	India	Greenbrier	8,903,000	China
Spotsylvania	15,349,000	India	Hampshire	3,145,000	India
Stafford	6,239,000	India	Hancock	21,766,000	India
Suffolk City	11,616,000	India	Hardy	2,237,000	India
Surry	856,000	India	Harrison	21,562,000	India
Sussex	2,023,000	India	Jackson	4,727,000	China
Tazewell	11,907,000	India	Jefferson	6,559,000	India
Virginia Beach City	53,260,000	India	Kanawha	69,764,000	China
Warren	5,184,000	India	Lewis	3,651,000	India
Washington	17,777,000	India	Lincoln	2,394,000	China
Westmoreland	2,933,000	India	Logan	5,215,000	China
Wise	9,646,000	India	McDowell	6,458,000	China
Wythe	6,709,000	India	Marion	20,127,000	India
York-Poquoson City	8,568,000	India	Marshall	9,845,000	India
			Mason	5,253,000	China
Washington	$ 924,958,000		Mercer	19,654,000	China
Adams	4,751,000	Japan	Mineral	6,029,000	India
Asotin	3,291,000	Japan	Mingo	4,233,000	China
Benton	34,258,000	Japan	Monongalia	13,428,000	India
Chelan	15,086,000	Korea, South	Monroe	2,606,000	China
Clallam	10,075,000	U.S.S.R.	Morgan	2,068,000	India
Clark	37,773,000	Korea, South	Nicholas	6,975,000	China
Columbia	1,317,000	Japan	Ohio	27,236,000	India
Cowlitz	18,213,000	Korea, South	Pendleton	1,766,000	India
Douglas	2,979,000	Japan	Pleasants	2,543,000	India
Ferry	406,000	Japan	Pocahontas	1,406,000	China
Franklin	9,277,000	Japan	Preston	5,479,000	India
Garfield	2,106,000	Japan	Putnam	5,398,000	China
Grant	10,044,000	Japan	Raleigh	17,397,000	China
Grays Harbor	12,068,000	U.S.S.R.	Randolph	4,986,000	India
Island	6,565,000	Korea, North	Ritchie	2,154,000	India
Jefferson	2,220,000	U.S.S.R.	Roane	2,473,000	China
King	312,644,000	Korea, North	Summers	2,063,000	China
	21,264,000	Korea, South	Taylor	3,429,000	India
Kitsap	28,871,000	U.S.S.R.	Tucker	1,557,000	India
Kittitas	3,900,000	Korea, South	Tyler	3,492,000	India
Klickitat	2,647,000	Korea, South	Upshur	3,811,000	India
Lewis	12,534,000	Korea, South	Wayne	6,474,000	China
Lincoln	5,219,000	Japan	Webster	1,186,000	China
Mason	4,153,000	U.S.S.R.	Wetzel	6,691,000	India
Okanogan	1,329,000	Japan	Wirt	1,116,000	China
	4,851,000	Korea, South	Wood	15,842,000	China
Pacific	2,505,000	Korea, South		15,159,000	India
Pend Oreille	1,107,000	Japan	Wyoming	4,890,000	China
Pierce	30,132,000	Korea, South			
	56,461,000	U.S.S.R.	Wisconsin	$ 2,169,464,000	
San Juan	787,000	Korea, North	Adams	1,425,000	China
Skagit	16,450,000	Korea, North	Ashland	7,388,000	China
Skamania	649,000	Korea, South	Barron	14,971,000	China
Snohomish	51,170,000	Korea, North	Bayfield	3,230,000	China
Spokane	79,171,000	Japan	Brown	94,112,000	China
Stevens	3,759,000	Japan	Buffalo	6,253,000	China
Thurston	25,531,000	U.S.S.R.	Burnett	2,264,000	China
Wahkiakum	429,000	Korea, South	Calumet	13,144,000	China
Walla Walla	15,927,000	Japan	Chippewa	18,997,000	China
Whatcom	19,795,000	Korea, North	Clark	13,256,000	China
Whitman	9,122,000	Japan	Columbia	24,046,000	China

U.S. County	U.S. Church Resources Available for Global Word and Deed Mission (Dollars)	Nation	U.S. County	U.S. Church Resources Available for Global Word and Deed Mission (Dollars)	Nation
Crawford	5,859,000	China	Rusk	4,478,000	China
Dane	137,941,000	China	St. Croix	17,694,000	China
Dodge	34,241,000	China	Sauk	22,124,000	China
Door	11,218,000	China	Sawyer	2,831,000	China
Douglas	13,673,000	China	Shawano	15,759,000	China
Dunn	10,206,000	China	Sheboygan	58,989,000	China
Eau Claire	30,592,000	China	Taylor	6,769,000	China
Florence	770,000	China	Trempealeau	12,150,000	China
Fond Du Lac	45,740,000	China	Vernon	9,977,000	China
Forest	1,936,000	China	Vilas	3,077,000	China
Grant	26,840,000	China	Walworth	21,702,000	China
Green	13,376,000	China	Washburn	3,054,000	China
Green Lake	10,726,000	China	Washington	40,440,000	China
Iowa	7,866,000	China	Waukesha	168,515,000	China
Iron	2,004,000	China	Waupaca	20,930,000	China
Jackson	5,072,000	China	Waushara	5,069,000	China
Jefferson	35,410,000	China	Winnebago	62,038,000	China
Juneau	7,383,000	China	Wood	36,401,000	China
Kenosha	53,534,000	China			
Kewaunee	10,244,000	China	Wyoming	$ 139,715,000	
La Crosse	40,470,000	China	Albany	6,438,000	China
Lafayette	9,421,000	China	Big Horn	2,694,000	China
Langlade	7,794,000	China	Campbell	6,162,000	China
Lincoln	11,207,000	China	Carbon	8,178,000	China
Manitowoc	43,488,000	China	Converse	2,799,000	China
Marathon	52,699,000	China	Crook	1,214,000	China
Marinette	15,002,000	China	Fremont	10,236,000	China
Marquette	3,641,000	China	Goshen	3,521,000	China
Menominee	621,000	China	Hot Springs	1,444,000	China
Milwaukee	449,751,000	China	Johnson	1,708,000	China
Monroe	13,124,000	China	Laramie	26,088,000	China
Oconto	11,030,000	China	Lincoln	1,163,000	China
Oneida	11,029,000	China	Natrona	29,803,000	China
Outagamie	77,341,000	China	Niobrara	831,000	China
Ozaukee	46,268,000	China	Park	7,300,000	China
Pepin	3,201,000	China	Platte	1,851,000	China
Pierce	10,415,000	China	Sheridan	7,799,000	China
Polk	11,401,000	China	Sublette	1,161,000	China
Portage	24,745,000	China	Sweetwater	11,186,000	China
Price	5,516,000	China	Teton	1,232,000	China
Racine	78,326,000	China	Uinta	1,209,000	China
Richland	4,520,000	China	Washakie	3,559,000	China
Rock	62,740,000	China	Weston	2,139,000	China

NOTES

Appendix A

1. Mid-1983 dollars.

2. Because Alaska has no counties, the 1980 census areas and boroughs that serve as county-equivalents for statistical reporting purposes were used in this entry (Source: *Churches and Church Membership in the United States, 1980,* Bernard Quinn, *et. al.,* Glenmary Research Center, Atlanta, Georgia, 1982, p. xiv).

3. As noted in *Churches and Church Membership in the United States 1980,* p. xiv, "In Virginia there are independent cities that are legally separate from the counties of that state. Since most denominations record location of churches within the counties from which these cities have been separated, it was decided to combine most of these cities with contiguous counties." Following is a listing of these combinations and exceptions which are employed in this Appendix A entry.

VIRGINIA INDEPENDENT CITY/COUNTY COMBINATIONS

Independent City	County	Abbreviation
Alexandria city *with*	Arlington	Arlington-Alexandria
Bedford city *with*	Bedford	Bedford-Bedford City
Bristol city *with*	Washington	Washington-Bristol
Buena Vista city *with*	Rockbridge	Rockbridge-Bn Vs-Lex
Charlottesville city *with*	Albemarle	Albemarle-Charlottes
Clifton Forge city *with*	Alleghany	Alleghany-Clf Fr-Cov
Colonial Heights city *with*	Dinwiddie	Dinwiddie-Col Ht-Pet
Covington city *with*	Alleghany	Alleghany-Clf Fr-Cov
Danville city *with*	Pittsylvania	Pittsylvania-Danvill
Emporia city *with*	Greensville	Greensville-Emporia
Fairfax city *with*	Fairfax	Fairfax-Fairfx-Fl Ch
Falls Church city *with*	Fairfax	Fairfax-Fairfx-Fl Ch
Franklin city *with*	Southampton	Southampton-Franklin
Fredericksburg city *with*	Spotsylvania	Spotsylvania-Frederi
Galax city *with*	Carroll	Carroll-Galax City
Harrisonburg city *with*	Rockingham	Rockingham-Harrison
Hopewell city *with*	Prince George	Prince George-Hopewe
Lexington city *with*	Rockbridge	Rockbridge-Bn Vs-Lex
Lynchburg city *with*	Campbell	Campbell-Lynchburg
Manassas city *with*	Prince William	Prince William-Manassas
Manassas Park city *with*	Prince William	Prince William-Manassas
Martinsville city *with*	Henry	Henry-Martinsville
Norton city *with*	Wise	Wise-Norton City
Petersburg city *with*	Dinwiddie	Dinwiddie-Col Ht-Pet
Poquoson city *with*	York	York-Poquoson City
Radford city *with*	Montgomery	Montgomery-Radford
Richmond city *with*	Henrico	Henrico-Richmond
Roanoke city *with*	Roanoke	Roanoke-Roanoke-Salm
Salem city *with*	Roanoke	Roanoke-Roanoke-Salm
South Boston city *with*	Halifax	Halifax-South Boston
Staunton city *with*	Augusta	Augusta-Staun-Waynes
Waynesboro city *with*	Augusta	Augusta-Staun-Waynes
Williamsburg city *with*	James City	James City-Williams
Winchester city *with*	Frederick	Frederick-Winchester

The only exceptions to the above pattern occur in the case of Independent Cities which have annexed their parent counties. These are usually treated as separate "city-county" combinations and are treated as such in this entry.

Independent City	Name
Hampton city	Hampton City
Newport News city	Newport News City
Norfolk city	Norfolk-Chesap-Ports
Chesapeake city	
Portsmouth city	
Suffolk city	Suffolk City (formerly Nansemond County)
Virginia Beach city	Virginia Beach City

SOURCE: *Churches and Church Membership in the United States 1980*, p. 316.

APPENDIX B
Yoking Map

Nations, Available U.S. Resources and U.S. State with Which Nation Is Matched

Resources Available for Global Word and Deed Mission[1] (Dollars)	Portion of Resources Available for Deed Mission[2] (Percent)	Nation	U.S. State
$ 456,470,000	90%	Afghanistan	New York
62,209,000	89%	Albania	New York
192,112,000	73%	Algeria	Connecticut
165,526,000	100%	Angola	Maine, New Hampshire
149,000	100%	Anguilla	Texas
1,108,000	100%	Antigua	Texas
59,751,000	100%	Argentina	Texas

Resources Available for Global Word and Deed Mission[1] (Dollars)	Portion of Resources Available for Deed Mission[2] (Percent)	Nation	U.S. State
1,039,000	0%	Bahrain	New York
2,720,004,000	91%	Bangladesh	Louisiana, Mississippi, Texas
2,409,000	100%	Belize	Texas
94,501,000	94%	Benin	New York
39,480,000	91%	Bhutan	Tennessee
125,118,000	100%	Bolivia	Texas
14,770,000	100%	Botswana	Maine
730,301,000	100%	Brazil	Texas
542,000	0%	Brunei	California
973,821,000	92%	Burma	Texas
108,419,000	100%	Burundi	Massachusetts
179,283,000	100%	Cameroon	New Hampshire, Vermont
8,175,000	100%	Cape Verde	New York
57,883,000	100%	Central African Republic	Masachusetts, Vermont
126,118,000	97%	Chad	Vermont
54,669,000	100%	Chile	Texas
$ 27,650,715,000	90%	China, People's Republic of	Arkansas, Colorado, Idaho, Illinois, Indiana, Iowa, Kansas, Kentucky, Michigan, Minnesota, Missouri, Montana, Nebraska, Nevada, North Dakota, Ohio, Oklahoma, South Dakota, Utah, West Virginia, Wisconsin, Wyoming
124,887,000	67%	China (Taiwan)	Oregon
6,000	0%	Christmas Island	Hawaii
6,000	95%	Cocos (Keeling) Islands	Hawaii
418,538,000	100%	Colombia	Texas
9,885,000	90%	Comoros	Massachusetts
31,688,000	100%	Congo	New Hampshire
244,000	100%	Cook Islands	Hawaii
21,110,000	100%	Costa Rica	Texas
133,131,000	93%	Cuba	Texas
8,990,000	91%	Djibouti	Rhode Island
1,813,000	100%	Dominica	Texas
88,670,000	99%	Dominican Republic	Texas
20,677,000	98%	East Timor	California
126,005,000	100%	Ecuador	Texas
954,607,000	93%	Egypt	New York
100,584,000	100%	El Salvador	Texas
9,048,000	100%	Equatorial Guinea	New Hampshire
852,106,000	100%	Ethiopia	Connecticut, Rhode Island
5,234,000	99%	Fiji	Hawaii
17,256,000	91%	Gambia	New York
280,312,000	100%	Ghana	New York
2,302,000	100%	Grenada	Texas
114,275,000	100%	Guatemala	Texas
153,578,000	90%	Guinea	New York
23,181,000	92%	Guinea-Bissau	New York
16,593,000	100%	Guyana	Texas
135,636,000	95%	Haiti	Texas
82,910,000	100%	Honduras	Texas
9,427,000	0%	Hong Kong	Oregon
19,265,193,000	91%	India	Alabama, Delaware, District of Columbia, Florida, Georgia, Maryland, Mississippi, New Jersey, North Carolina,

Resources Available for Global Word and Deed Mission[1] (Dollars)	Portion of Resources Available for Deed Mission[2] (Percent)	Nation	U.S. State
			Pennsylvania, South Carolina, Tennessee, Virginia West Virginia
3,825,038,000	92%	Indonesia	California
265,025,000	62%	Iran	New York
32,179,000	0%	Iraq	New York
10,720,000	0%	Israel	New York
146,173,000	94%	Ivory Coast	New York
37,703,000	100%	Jamaica	Texas
322,775,000	0%	Japan	Hawaii, Washington
63,804,000	87%	Jordan	New York
207,612,000	91%	Kampuchea	Arizona, California
380,782,000	100%	Kenya	Massachusetts Rhode Island
1,180,000	100%	Kiribati	Hawaii
407,411,000	88%	Korea, North	Washington
496,986,000	91%	Korea, South	Oregon, Washington
3,331,000	0%	Kuwait	New York
112,209,000	91%	Laos	Arizona
33,534,000	100%	Lebanon	New York
32,598,000	100%	Lesotho	Maine
44,023,000	96%	Liberia	New York
8,247,000	0%	Libya	Connecticut
2,714,000	75%	Macao	Oregon
217,192,000	100%	Madagascar	Massachusetts
155,651,000	100%	Malawi	Massachusetts
169,510,000	81%	Malaysia	California
4,407,000	90%	Maldives	Florida
202,873,000	91%	Mali	New York
45,755,000	90%	Mauritania	New York
17,098,000	95%	Mauritius	Massachusetts
1,359,000	90%	Mayotte	Massachusetts
352,878,000	100%	Mexico	Texas
31,708,000	85%	Mongolia	Idaho
162,000	100%	Montserrat	Texas
440,925,000	87%	Morocco	Connecticut, New York
277,148,000	97%	Mozambique	Massachusetts
13,351,000	100%	Namibia	Maine
426,466,000	91%	Nepal	Tennessee
55,087,000	100%	Nicaragua	Texas
147,276,000	90%	Niger	New York
1,486,155,000	99%	Nigeria	New York
50,000	100%	Niue Island	Hawaii
2,467,000	0%	Oman	New York
2,197,000	100%	Pacific Islands (Trust Territory)	Hawaii
2,301,005,000	90%	Pakistan	New York, Pennsylvania
17,504,000	100%	Panama	Texas
60,143,000	100%	Papua New Guinea	Hawaii
42,399,000	100%	Paraguay	Texas
325,403,000	100%	Peru	Texas
987,184,000	100%	Philippines	California, Oregon
27,240,000	100%	Portugal	New York
569,000	0%	Qatar	New York
61,669,000	100%	Romania	New York
134,909,000	100%	Rwanda	Massachusetts
100,000	100%	St. Helena	New Hampshire
923,000	100%	St. Kitts-Nevis	Texas
2,404,000	100%	St. Lucia	Texas
2,436,000	100%	St. Vincent	Texas
3,408,000	100%	Samoa, Western	Hawaii
2,643,000	100%	Sao Tome & Principe	New Hampshire
24,814,000	0%	Saudi Arabia	New York
148,065,000	91%	Senegal	New York
609,000	100%	Seychelles	Massachusetts

Resources Available for Global Word and Deed Mission[1] (Dollars)	Portion of Resources Available for Deed Mission[2] (Percent)	Nation	U.S. State
97,278,000	92%	Sierra Leone	New York
5,148,000*	0%	Singapore	California
5,426,000	100%	Solomon Islands	Hawaii
135,551,000	90%	Somalia	Rhode Island
99,124,000	100%	South Africa	Maine
414,844,000	92%	Sri Lanka	Florida
474,847,000	91%	Sudan	Connecticut
11,826,000	100%	Swaziland	Maine
146,403,000	86%	Syria	New York
474,484,000	99%	Tanzania	Massachusetts
1,114,961,000	89%	Thailand	Arizona, New Mexico, Texas
61,713,000	97%	Togo	New York
38,000	100%	Tokelau	Hawaii
2,209,000	100%	Tonga	Hawaii
107,535,000	84%	Tunisia	Connecticut
697,856,000	82%	Turkey	New York
78,000	100%	Turks & Caicos Islands	Texas
180,000	100%	Tuvalu	Hawaii
337,153,000	100%	Uganda	Massachusetts
246,175,000	0%	Union of Soviet Socialist Republics (U.S.S.R.)	Alaska Washington
2,198,000	0%	United Arab Emirates	New York
164,061,000	93%	Upper Volta	New York
2,664,000	100%	Vanuatu	Hawaii
1,554,416,000	92%	Viet Nam	California
148,000	100%	Wallis & Futuna Islands	Hawaii
2,866,000	87%	Western Sahara	New York
153,803,000	89%	Yemen, North	New York
50,945,000	90%	Yemen, South	New York
739,961,000	100%	Zaire	Massachusetts
129,521,000	100%	Zambia	Massachusetts
161,583,000	100%	Zimbabwe	Massachusetts

NOTES

Appendix B

1. Resources listed in this column are additional overseas mission funds potentially available from U.S. Christians annually at the 10 percent giving level for each nation in 1983 U.S. Dollars.

2. The *Portion* Column indicates what percentage of the resources available for a given country could be applied to deed mission efforts, the remaining percentage of resources being applied directly to increasing evangelistic efforts.

To apply this column, the dollar amount for a given country listed under the Resources Column can be multiplied by the percentage under the *Portion* Column. The resulting number indicates the suggested additional cash amount available for deed mission in that country. The dollar amount suggested for word missions is obtained by subtracting the deed dollar amount from the total dollar amount allocated for a given country. Similarly, the percentage of resources assumed for word missions is merely 100 minus the percentage given in the *Portion* Column.

A few qualifications are in order concerning those instances in which 100 percentage is allocated for deed mission.

First, it should be remembered that these instances result from situations in which it is estimated that there are at least 50 percent Christians in that country.

Second, it is not suggested that there is no evangelism need in those countries. Rather, these instances result from situations in which it is estimated that there are at least 50 percent Christians in such a country and that for the most part there is likely the wherewithal within the church in such countries to spread the Good News of Jesus Christ.

Third, it must be clearly borne in mind that this allocation schedule is presented with regard to new funds resulting from increased giving levels. Therefore, in the event that denominational or paradenominational mission agencies presently allocate funds for work in a given country, these funds would continue to be available for that word mission work over and above the allocations presented in Appendix B.

Fourth, if either increased word or deed mission funds are deemed necessary over and above the current amount given through denominational and paradenominational mission agencies, and over and above the additional new amounts suggested in Appendix B at the 10 percent giving level, two options come to mind. On the one hand, average giving will hopefully increase above the 10 percent level which would provide additional funds for either word and deed mission. On the other hand, these percentages are only recommendations; thus the actual percentage breakdown between word and deed missions can be determined by Christians in an area presumably upon consultation with various denominational and paradenominational mission agencies in the U.S. as well as with representatives of the church in the specific nation under discussion.

Fifth, since we are after all considering deed mission and not governmental development, it may be assumed that some portion of the funds budgeted for deed mission would go either for integration with word missions of the national church or for general interpretation of the deed mission in line with the Good News of Jesus Christ. This factor might be of particular importance in countries where the percent Christian is over 50 percent and thus the portion allocated in Appendix B for deed mission is 100 percent.

Sixth, it should be borne in mind that, as pointed out earlier, presumably development, and therefore deed mission, by its very definition, is proportionately more expensive than word mission. This will be reflected in the percentages allocated for deed mission which generally run higher than those allocated for word mission in Appendix B. However, as noted previously, the higher 10:1 weighting of allocations for deed missions does not reflect the relative importance of deed and word missions.

Seventh, and last, by way of an overview summary, it is of interest to note that the word missions allocations suggested by the percentages in the *Portion* Column call for an additional $7,289,623,000 for word missions annually over what is currently being given. This additional $7.3 billion dollars is allocated so that it is focused on areas where there are fewer than 50 percent Christians.

SCRIPTURE INDEX

GENERAL INDEX

About the authors —

Sylvia Ronsvalle graduated with high honors and Phi Beta Kappa from the University of Illinois, Urbana-Champaign, receiving a B.A. in 1971.

John Ronsvalle received a B.A. from Syracuse University ('60), attended Fuller Theological Seminary (S.T.B. '63) and received his M.A. ('65) and Ph.D. ('72) in Clinical Psychology from the University of Illinois, Urbana-Champaign.

Together they founded *empty tomb, inc.,* and have been working fulltime as Coordinator and Facilitator respectively, since 1972, offering discipleship opportunities to members of Champaign County. The outreaches include food, clothing and furniture distribution, home repair, placing an R.N. at a local health clinic, a monthly dinner to bring Christians together across racial, economic and denominational barriers, the co-operative Bread from Jesus focus on Northeast Brazil and a magazine published for the body of Christ in the Champaign-Urbana area.